Cultural Distance in International Ventures

Katiuscia Vaccarini · Francesca Spigarelli
Ernesto Tavoletti · Christoph Lattemann

Cultural Distance in International Ventures

Exploring Perceptions of European and Chinese Managers

palgrave
macmillan

Katiuscia Vaccarini
Free University of Bozen-Bolzano
Bolzano, Italy

Ernesto Tavoletti
University of Macerata
Macerata, Italy

Francesca Spigarelli
University of Macerata
Macerata, Italy

Christoph Lattemann
Jacobs University
Bremen, Germany

ISBN 978-3-319-62192-0 ISBN 978-3-319-62193-7 (eBook)
DOI 10.1007/978-3-319-62193-7

Library of Congress Control Number: 2017948258

Cover illustration: Pattern adapted from an Indian cotton print produced in the 19th century

Printed on acid-free paper

This Palgrave Macmillan imprint is published by Springer Nature
The registered company is Springer International Publishing AG
The registered company address is: Gewerbestrasse 11, 6330 Cham, Switzerland

Contents

List of Tables

1
Introduction

Abstract In this book, we investigate the concept of "distance", in particular the concepts of "cultural distance" and "psychic distance" in international business contexts. We particularly focus on the green tech industry and Sino-European FDI. We analyze managers' perceived distance (measured on twelve dimensions such as culture, language, political system, and business practices) between the firm's home country and the firm's host country (Child et al. 2009). After introducing the concept of psychic distance and the context of our research, we present in the second chapter a systematic literature review on psychic distance as a factor for FDI motivation and location decisions. Chapter 3 follows up on the relevance of culture and cultural differences in international business and illustrates how insights from the field of social psychology may help to overcome cultural pitfalls in international business and how to manage cultural conflicts. The fourth chapter explores managers' perceptions of psychic distances in the context of European green tech FDI to China by applying a multiple-case study research design. Our analyses show that managers' perceptions of psychic distances vary over time, i.e., between the points in time before managers enter a market and after they have entered the market. In Chap. 5, we examine the

K. Vaccarini et al., *Cultural Distance in International Ventures*,
DOI 10.1007/978-3-319-62193-7_1

relevance of Chinese managers' perceived distance for their FDI decisions and the changes of their perceptions after entering a foreign market and after gaining experiences in operating in the host country. Here, we particularly focus on Chinese FDI flows in the green tech sector to Europe, with a country focus on Germany, by presenting six case studies. This analysis shows that managers, with and without experiences in foreign markets, should not depend their FDI decision on their perceptions of differences between countries. This book ends with concluding remarks and a summary of the research findings. The presented research is part of an EU Marie Curie project on *Partnering Opportunities between Europe and China in the Renewable Energy and Environmental iNdustry* (POREEN[1]).

Keywords PD · Psychic distance · Dimensions · Managers' perceptions · Cultural distance · Cultural pitfalls · International business · Green tech industry · Sino-European FDI · European investments · European Marie Curie project

The significant role of "distance" for international business, in practice as well as in research, can be summarized with a sentence: "International management is management of distance" (Zaheer et al. 2012: 19).

In research, perceived distance in cross-border business is either operationalized by the construct of "cultural distance" or by the construct of "psychic distance". Psychic distance comprises twelve dimensions, one of them is cultural distance, and is hence the more comprehensive concept. Psychic distance is defined as the existing perceived distance between the characteristics of the firm's home country and the characteristics of the firm's host country (Child et al. 2009). This construct is also related to dimensions such as geographical distance, language, level of education, level of economic development, level of technological development, logistical infrastructures, political system, legal system, regulations, accepted business practices, and business ethics (Child et al. 2009).

Over the past decades, a growing body of literature on psychic distance has emerged. The term psychic distance has been first coined by Beckerman (1956) in his analysis of factors that aims at explaining trade and investment flows between countries. The Uppsala scholars (Johanson and Vahlne 1977, 2009) and Dunning (1980) conducted in-depth studies on firms' internationalization by applying psychic distance in their models. Some other studies also referred to the concept of psychic distance (Wei and Alon 2010; Chen and Chen 1998); however, this concept seems to have been widely ignored by the larger mainstream FDI literature.

Recent studies draw much attention on the "psychic" rather than the "distance" concept of the construct by focusing on the cognitive aspects and individual perceptions. We follow this trend in research and, in this book, incorporate literature on distance and perceptions in international business and adopt an interdisciplinary approach by applying some social psychological theoretical foundations to analyze and interpret cross-cultural business dynamics, such as social identity, ethnocentrism, and intergroup relations (Sumner 1906; Turner 1975; Brewer 2003).

This book uses both the concept of cultural distance and the concept of psychic distance, to analyze managers' perceived distances, their changes over time, and the impact of perceived distance on FDI decisions. This book shows results from several sectorial studies and focuses on the green tech sector in a Sino-European business environment.

Over the past decades, China has become the largest recipient of FDI in the developing world and is now the second largest recipient of FDI globally, after USA (Coughlin and Segev 2000; Zhang 2001). Even more striking is that in the past decade, China has begun to invert the trend of its investment flows, gaining place in the global scenario being a source of outbound FDI (Spigarelli 2009, 2010). Since 2013, China is also the largest source of FDI outflow in the developing and transition economies and ranks number two worldwide (UNCTAD 2014).

In recent years, the combination of the increasing environmental awareness in China and the economic recession in Europe has created a climate, which, in particular, is increasingly conducive to Chinese OFDI in the green tech industry (Lv and Spigarelli 2016). China has been devoting increasing attention to environmental issues and pollution reduction. A wide and comprehensive "green policy" has been embedded in the recent China's Five-Year Plans. Policy measures in China embrace a series of sectors (Langer and Watson 2004; Aawa and Yang 2010; Huang and Chen 2015) and include strict targets for emission reductions and increased use of renewable energies. In particular, China is continuing to support the green tech industry by devoting gradual emphasis on environmental issues since the Sixth Five-Year Plan (Hu 2014).

In Europe, since the recession in 2008, critiques on public spending have forced many governments to reduce their public support in the renewable energy sector. This is why European firms are more and more open for joint ventures, strategic alliances, or merge with foreign firms, often with firms from emerging markets (Lv and Spigarelli 2015). Recent studies on the integration of European and Chinese green tech markets (Curran 2015; Lv and Spigarelli 2015, 2016) report that Europe has become an important destination for sales from Chinese global green firms. Among them, Germany is one of the world's largest investors in the renewable energy sector and is a popular destination to Chinese OFDI (e.g., Schütte and Chen 2012; Lv and Spigarelli 2016). This is why we focus our analyses on perceptions of European managers investing in China and on individual perceptions of Chinese managers investing in Europe in the renewable energy sector.

We did that by interviewing Chinese and European managers to get information about their perception of distances toward their respective host country. We asked managers to rate their perceived *differences* between their home country and the particular host country along each of the twelve psychic distance dimensions. We further asked them about the perceived *impact* that each dimension has on conducting business with the host country. The in-depth study of managers' perceptions derives from their crucial role as decision-makers, whose perceptions and skills in facing psychic distance determine the success, the performances, or the failure of the firm's internationalization process (Harzing 2003; Brewer 2007; Child et al. 2009; Hashim 2012).

Our findings show that cultural distance is one of the most relevant dimensions of psychic distance (among the aforementioned twelve dimensions) for FDI decision making. The study results also show that the managers' perceptions of *differences* regarding the legal framework, regulations, and business ethics are changing quite sharply over time (after managers gather experiences in the foreign market), and that the perceived *impact* of differences on business decision needs corrections over time. Hence, both distance concepts can be categorized as "non-economic" or "intangible" factors, which influence FDI (location) decisions.

After this introductory chapter, this book is organized into four chapters and a concluding summary. Chapter 2 presents a systematic literature review on psychic distance. The aim is to investigate whether and to what extent psychic distance is considered as a determinant of FDI in the context of Chinese international business relationships. Chapter 3 builds on the literature review and analysis of managers' perceptions of cultural distance in general. We show that perceptions of cultural distance bias managers decision making and that managers should be aware of the importance of their own perception of cultural differences in conducting international business. The emphasis is on the advantages and opportunities that differences between home and host country can generate. This can be achieved by setting up an intercultural laboratory as a "structured business practice" in the company organization. This chapter pinpoints the *sociocognitive* value of this kind of laboratory which is structured on a group basis and addressed to early step international managers. This chapter aims at fostering the "dialogue" between different cultures and, in a parallel way, between different academic research areas. A social psychological perspective is adopted to interpret and analyze the international business context under examination. Chapter 4 aims at analyzing European managers' perceptions of cultural differences between their home country and the far-distant country China in the context of green tech FDI. We emphasize on "host-bound" identity perceptions of European managers toward the Chinese marketplace. Our results show that European managers' perceptions of cultural distances vary with their experiences of operating in China and that, consequently, their perceptions change after they entered the Chinese market. In fact, before the interviewed managers entered the Chinese market (pre-market entry period) they did not consider cultural differences between their home country and China as relevant for conducting business. However, after the managers entered the Chinese market, they realized its crucial role for international business. Further, as about "host-bound" perceptions of identity, European managers seem to perceive China as a single identity and do not perceive differences within the country in the pre-market entry period. In Chap. 5, we applied the concept of psychic distance (as a broader concept than cultural distance) to the context of green tech Chinese OFDI to Germany. This chapter broadens the perspective and examines differences on twelve dimensions in the Sino-German business context. We show to what extent managers' perceptions of the twelve psychic distance dimensions per se change over time and how the perceived impact of these twelve dimensions change over time. This research has several contributions, which will be illustrated and discussed in the summarizing conclusion (Chap. 6).

Note

1. The EU funded project is POREEN—*Partnering Opportunities between Europe and China in the Renewable Energies and Environmental iNdustries*—European Union's Seventh Framework Programme FP7/2007–2013/under REA grant agreement no 318908. The project is coordinated by University of Macerata, Italy.

References

Aiwa, M., & Yang, C. (2010). Green credit, green stimulus, green revolution? China's mobilization of banks for environmental cleanup. *The Journal of Environment and Development, 19*(2), 119–144.

Beckerman, W. (1956). Distance and the pattern of intra-European trade. *The Review of Economics and Statistics, 38*(31), 31–40.

Brewer, M. B. (2003). *Intergroup relations.* Berkshire: Free University Press.

Brewer, P. (2007). Psychic distance and Australian export market selection. *Australian Journal of Management, 32*(1), 73–94.

Chen, H., & Chen, T.-J. (1998). Network linkages and location choice in foreign direct investment. *Journal of International Business Studies, 29*(3), 445–467.

Child, J., Rodrigues, S. B., & Frynas, J. G. (2009). Psychic distance, its impact and coping modes: Interpretations of SMEs decision-makers. *Management International Review, 49*(2), 199–224.

Coughlin, C. C., & Segev, E. (2000). Foreign direct investment in China: A spatial econometric study. *The World Economy, 3*(1), 1–23.

Curran, L. (2015). The impact of trade policy on global production networks: The solar panel case. *Review of International Political Economy*. Available at: http://dx.doi.org/10.1080/09692290.2015.1014927. Accessed Apr 2017.

Dunning, J. H. (1980). Toward an eclectic theory of international production: Some empirical tests. *Journal of International Business Studies, 11*(1), 9–31.

Harzing, A. W. (2003). The role of culture in entry-mode studies: From neglect to myopia? In J. L. C. Cheng & M. A. Hitt (Eds.), *Managing multinationals in a knowledge economy: Economics culture advances in international management, 15*, 75–127. Emerald Group: Bingley.

Hashim, F. (2012). Outward internationalization and FDI: Motives for Malaysian MNEs moving into China. *Review of Business & Finance Studies, 3*(2), 89–102.

Hu, A. (2014). *China: Innovative green development*. Berlin, Heidelberg: Springer Verlag.

Huang, R., & Chen, D. (2015). Does environmental information disclosure benefit waste discharge reduction? Evidence from China. *Journal of Business Ethics, 129*(3), 535–552.

Johanson, J., & Vahlne, E. (1977). The internationalization process of the firm: A model of knowledge development and increasing foreign market commitments. *Journal of International Business Studies, 8*, 23–32.

Johanson, J., & Vahlne, E. (2009). The Uppsala internationalization process model revisited: From liability of foreignness to liability of outsidership. *Journal of International Business Studies, 40*(9), 1411–1431.

Langer, K., & Watson, R. (2004). The greening of China's building industry. *China Business Review, 31*(6), 56–63.

Lv, P., & Spigarelli, F. (2015). The integration of Chinese and European renewable energy markets: The role of Chinese foreign direct investments. *Energy Policy, 81*, 14–26.

Lv, P., & Spigarelli, F. (2016). The determinants of location choice: Chinese foreign direct investments in the European renewable energy sector. *International Journal of Emerging Markets*, forthcoming.

Schütte, H., & Chen, S. (2012). Reaching high: Sany's internationalization (A) and (B). *China Europe International Business School*, case CC-312-019, case CC-312-020.

Spigarelli, F. (2009). *Le multinazionali dei paesi emergenti: Gli investimenti cinesi in Italia* [MNEs from emerging countries: Chinese investment in Italy. With English summary]. *Economia Politica e Industriale, 36*(2), 131–159.

Spigarelli, F. (2010). Chinese investments in Italy: Is the wave arriving? *International Journal of Asian Business and Information Management, 1*(1), 54–76.

Sumner, W. G. (1906). *Folksways*. New York: Ginn.

Turner, J. C. (1975). Social comparison and social identity: Some prospects for intergroup behaviour. *European Journal of Social Psychology, 5*, 5–34.

UNCTAD. (2014, January 28). *Global investment trends monitor*. (No 15). New York: United Nations.

Wei, W., & Alon, I. (2010). Chinese outward direct investment: A study on macroeconomic determinants. *International Journal and Emerging Markets, 2*(4), 352–369.

Zaheer, S., Schomaker, M. S., & Nachum, L. (2012). Distance without direction: Restoring credibility to a much-loved construct. *Journal of International Business Studies, 43*, 18–27.

Zhang, K. H. (2001). China's inward FDI boom and the greater Chinese economy. *The Chinese Economy, 34*(1), 74–88.

2
Psychic Distance and FDI: The Case of China

Abstract This chapter seeks to investigate whether and to what extent Psychic Distance (PD) is considered by scholars as a specific determinant of inbound and outbound foreign direct investments (FDIs) in China. The key finding of the study is that psychic distance as a determinant influencing FDI seems to be under-investigated. This chapter also aims to systematize the limited and fragmented literature about non-tangible perceptions of "distance" between home and host economies and contributes to raising awareness on the concept of psychic distance. It provides useful insights and practical implications for various interest groups such as international business scholars (a more comprehensive review and systematization of the concept of psychic distance), managers (awareness raising on psychic distance, opportunities and challenges in the IB scenario, and setting up and strengthening long-term cooperation between Europe and China), and policy makers (investment flows between Europe and China and key barriers which

This paper has been previously published in the Journal of Comparative International Management: Vaccarini, K. (2015), "Psychic distance and FDI: The case of China," *Journal of Comparative International Management*, Vol. 18, No. 1, pp. 1–23. Reprinted with permission from the Journal of Comparative International Management.

K. Vaccarini et al., *Cultural Distance in International Ventures*,
DOI 10.1007/978-3-319-62193-7_2

affect companies and require action politically and institutionally to ensure that opportunities are fully exploited by companies).

Keywords PD · Psychic distance · Cultural distance · Determinant FDI · China · Managers' perceptions · International business Uppsala OLI · OLMA · LLL · Hofstede · Cross · Cultural Cross-country · Cross border · Psychic distance dimensions Geographical distance · Level of education · Level of economic development Level of technological development · Political system Legal system · Regulations · Accepted business practices · Business ethics

1 Introduction[1]

There is considerable literature on foreign direct investment (FDI) in China. However, the issue of Psychic Distance (PD) as a determinant of FDI has been poorly addressed (Wei and Alon 2010; Cheng and Kwan 2000; Zhang 2000). This study proposes a systematic review of the literature about whether and to what extent psychic distance affects FDI, with respect to China–Europe and Europe–China bilateral relationships. Key questions to be answered are the following: Is psychic distance a key FDI determinant, especially in China/Asian context? Does it affect the decision-making and the internationalization processes of firms? Is psychic distance being considered in models assessing FDI? Are there specific studies in the international business literature which investigate psychic distance as one of the determinants of FDI in China?

1.1 Perception and Interpretation of the New Environment

First of all, a general introduction to psychic distance in the field of IB is necessary. On the basis of the definition adopted by Johanson and Vahlne (1977, 2009) and others (e.g., Dow and Karunaratna 2006), psychic distance can be considered as the perception of similarities and differences between home and host countries. The concept of psychic distance is strictly related to cultural distance (Child et al. 2009).

When local firms decide to go international, it gets more complex in terms of economic, cultural, and political dimensions than in the home country, not to mention the presence of the uncertainty factor. The literature supports the importance of the cultural and the political dimensions along with the economic one (Markusen 1995). However, such an environment may not adequately fit in the theories explaining the behavior of multinational enterprises (MNEs), international or global firms, and FDI Hosseini (2005). Theories that have emerged after Hymer's study (Hymer 1960)[2] focus on economic and tangible features. But these theories would be incomplete if cultural and political dimensions would not be considered.

Hosseini (2005) goes beyond traditional FDI theory to emphasize the importance of behavioral economics. He suggests to utilize the behaviorally based model developed by Heiner (1985) in explaining FDI decisions since the reality of international environment faced by managers—economic, cultural, and political—seems to reflect the behavioral economics theories. Accordingly, MNEs are seen as complex organizations and their decision-makers as boundedly rational real human beings. Each of them possesses different capacities to interpret information relevant to the FDI decision process (Hosseini 2005). What he argues is strongly related to the psychic distance perceptions as it covers such topics as subjective interpretation of the environment, similarities and differences.

1.2 Relevance of the Topic and Gaps in the Extant Literature

The internationalization process (Johanson and Vahlne 1977, 2009) presupposes to develop a deep understanding of the cultural environment in the respective host country, and this point seems to be underestimated by FDI research and practice (Hosseini 2005). Lenartowicz and Roth (1999) suggest that IB scholars generally recognize that culture is an important construct and that the field is in need of additional understanding about culture and its effects. For example, Dunning (1980, 2001, 2009.) argues that firms which are best able to identify and reconcile (cultural) difference, or even exploit them to their gain, are likely to acquire a noticeable competitive advantage in the marketplace.

The perceptions of distance could be practically translated into additional costs: The greater the corporate headquarters and subsidiaries differ in their cultural characteristics, the more difficult it becomes to effectively supervise the various units. Drawing from earlier work by Kogut and Singh (1988), some scholars depict the headquarter–subsidiary relationship as "agency" (Roth and O'Donnell 1996). Thus, it can be derived that the cost of this agency increases because they have to face cultural distance (Gomez-Mejia and Polick 1997).

Perceptions of "distances" are captured not only by the concept of psychic distance, which embraces more than the distance perceptions related to culture, but also to other areas such as, geographical distance, language, level of education, level of economic development, level of technological development, political system, legal system, regulations, accepted business practices, and business ethics (Child et al. 2009). This literature review embraces Child et al.'s (2009) definition of psychic distance. Accordingly, psychic distance is defined as the existing perceived distance between home and host country's characteristics (Child et al. 2009). The concepts of psychic distance and of cultural distance should be kept separated, although they are both "non-economic" and "non-tangible" factors.

To sum up, existing research on FDI determinants tends to focus on economic or standard factors, such as market size and trade openness (Chakrabarti 2001; Hong et al. 2001; Hong 2007; Zheng 2011). Ma et al. (2008) use the concept of openness as the sum of exports and imports divided by GDP and not in terms of acceptance of foreign values, behavior, or rules. The majority of the articles reviewed in this chapter contains a low number of references to psychic distance as a factor influencing FDI (Xiaojuan et al. 2004; Ma et al. 2008).

First of all, this work aims at filling the gap in the IB literature by investigating if non economic factors, specifically psychic distance, are considered by scholars as an FDI determinant. Second, this chapter investigates how many studies on psychic distance are related to the Chinese marketplace. First, an approach based on the interaction between non economic factors (e.g., differences in religion, language or cultural distance, and psychic distance) and economic factors are a matter of concern to investors in their location choice decisions. Second, FDI is widely viewed as beneficial for host country's economic development since it is a vehicle for carrying finance and transferring advanced intangible assets—knowledge, technical, and management skills.[3] Furthermore, a low level of psychic distance enables companies to carry out a correct and responsible management of their international activities, and they can benefit from it in the long run.

For FDI-seeking policy makers, an in-depth understanding of the underlying drivers of FDI helps design of policies to improve the country's future performance, especially the intangible FDI determinants. For example, most studies on FDI recognize the role of language as a component of cultural, psychic, and administrative distance (Dow and Karunaratna 2006). Subsequently, factors affecting the location of FDI–both economic and non economic—can provide guidance to policy makers in identifying not only the obstacles that some regions must overcome to attract FDI (Coughlin and Segev 2000; Zhang 2001b), but also opportunities and knowledge to exploit (Dunning 2000). FDI may depend on other FDI in proximate countries (Li et al. 2008). Such spatial interdependence may be complementary to non-spatial determinants, which in turn go hand in hand with non economic or non-tangible factors. These drivers seem to have been ignored by the mainstream literature on the determinants of FDI, with only few studies dealing with such topics as psychic distance or psychologically close investors and markets (Wei and Alon 2010; Chen and Chen 1998).

1.3 China: Current Trends in the Worldwide Business Scenario

From an almost isolated economy in 1979, China has become the largest recipient of FDI in the developing world, and globally, the second after the USA for many years (Coughlin and Segev 2000; Zhang 2001a). Most importantly, China has recently begun to invert the trend of its investment flows, gaining place in the global scenario being a source of outbound FDI (Spigarelli 2009, 2010). According to the

United Nation Conference on Trade and Development (2014), China ranked first in the developing and transition economies and second in the world with inflows at an estimated US$127 billion—including both financial and non-financial sectors (UNCTAD 2014). In the Association of Southeast Asian Nations (ASEAN), FDI growth slowed down, yet prospects for this region continue to be promising since more FDI arrive from China and Japan in a wide range of sectors, including infrastructure, finance, and manufacturing. China is one of the countries which largely drove inflows to rise in 2013 following a surge in FDI. It is particularly responsible for the rise in cross-border merger and acquisition sales in 2013, mainly driven by deals in East and Southeast Asia. FDI flows could have risen further in 2014 and 2015 to US$1.8 trillion (UNCTAD 2014).

This chapter is structured as follows. Section 2 provides a theoretical background including the FDI theory milestones, and the most applied frameworks focused on distance perceptions and some remarks on the most recent trends regarding institutional theory are also included. In Sect. 3, the article's selection and classification methodologies are explained. Section 4 provides the analysis of the main findings and Sect. 5 their discussions. Section 6 concludes this chapter with remarks on avenues for future research, policy implications, and limitations of the present study.

2 Theoretical Background

Contributions to the literature focusing on FDI determinants could be divided into two major research streams: the micro perspective includes such contributions as transaction cost theory, internationalization theory, and the eclectic paradigm, and the macro perspective contributions like orthodox trade theory, Kemp-MacDougall theory and product life cycle theory, and Heckscher-Ohlin-Samuelson paradigm (Samuelson 1948). The microeconomic viewpoint tries to explain the motivations for investment across boundaries. Moreover, it examines the consequences for investors, for the country of origin, and for the host country rather than investment flows and stock. From a macroeconomic point of view, FDI is considered a particular form of capital flows across borders, which is found in the balance of payments and has such variables as capital flows and stocks, revenues obtained from investments (Vintila 2010). Regarding the macro perspective, on the one hand, FDI effects are often seen as generators of employment, high productivity, competitiveness, and technology spillovers. Especially for the least developed countries, FDI is synonym of exports, access to international markets and international currencies. On the other hand, FDI may have a negative impact on economic development. The positive or negative effects potentially depend on the nature of the sector in which the investment takes place (Vintila 2010).

The main contributions to FDI theory can be highlighted as follows (Hosseini 2005; Vintila 2010; Bartels et al. 2014): production life cycle theory, theory of exchange rate on imperfect capital markets, the internationalization theory, and the eclectic paradigm as summarized in Table 1.

As shown in Table 1, since every new evidence developed over the years has added some new elements and criticisms to the previous contributions, we cannot identify a generally accepted theory. However, Dunning's OLI (1980) remains the dominant operational framework within IB to understand FDI motivations and location choices (Bartels et al. 2014). Of course, the original model was further developed over the years.[4]

2.1 Psychic Distance, Internationalization, and FDI

Empirical literature indicates that exchange rates, market size, government policies and incentives, political risk, cost of labor, labor skills, trade openness and export orientation policy, and infrastructure are the key determinants of FDI (Zhang 2001a, b; Fung et al. 2005; Chantasasawat et al. 2010). However, two of the most applicable theories that are considered in this work provide details in the internationalization process, such as the Uppsala model (Johanson and Vahlne 1977, 2009) and Dunning's eclectic paradigm (Dunning 1980, etc.). In particular, the eclectic paradigm includes details regarding inbound and outbound FDI determinants.

Table 1 Milestones in FDI theory

Author	Year	Theoretical model	Model application
Vernon	1966	Production life cycle theory	The four stages of production life cycle—innovation, growth, maturity, and decline—explained certain types of FDI made by US companies in Western Europe between 1950 and 1970 in the manufacturing industry
Cushman	1985	Theory of exchange rates on imperfect capital markets	Analysis of the foreign exchange risk from the perspective of international trade. The author analyzed the influence of uncertainty as a factor of FDI. Real exchange rate increase stimulated US FDI, while a foreign currency appreciation has reduced American FDI
Buckley and Casson[a]	1976	The internationalization theory	Demonstration that transnational companies grow and are motivated to achieve FDI by organizing their internal activities so as to develop specific advantages, which can then to be exploited

(continued)

Table 1 (continued)

Author	Year	Theoretical model	Model application
Dunning	1980	The eclectic paradigm (OLI)	OLI eclectic paradigm (ownership, location and internationalization advantages) shows that OLI parameters are different from company to company and depend on context and reflect the economic, political, and social characteristics of the host country

[a]The internationalization theory was initially launched by Coase (1937) in a national context and by Hymer (1960) in an international context. After its elaboration by Buckley and Casson (1976), the theory was further developed by Hennart (1982).

These two theoretical frameworks have a common feature which is relevant to this study: the presence of the psychic distance construct. Psychic distance appears firstly in the 1950s when Beckerman (1956) and later Linnemann (1966) started to examine the concept, paving the way to and raising interest in the fields of IB and international management. Beckerman demonstrates that psychic distance influences trade patterns. He refers to economic distance in terms of transport costs and suggests that psychic distance is meaningful in the form of gaining knowledge of foreign markets through personal contacts. Some scholars define psychic distance as geography or transport costs (Linnemann 1966; Leamer 1974), while others (Gruber and Vernon 1970) argue that the concept should not be identified with transport costs alone. Instead, it should incorporate knowledge about sources and markets.

The appreciation of psychic distance as a determinant of FDI, for example in Dunning's eclectic paradigm (Dunning 1980), is preceded by a dominance of internationalization theory attributing to psychic distance a fundamental role in the four-stage internationalization process developed by the Uppsala school (Johanson and Vahlne 1977). In order to adjust to the changes in the firm and in its environment, internationalization consists in a series of incremental steps. Psychic distance is the main determinant in this model, and it is defined as the sum of factors preventing the flow of information from and to the market (Johanson and Vahlne 1977). This definition entails such differences between home and host country as language, education, business practices, culture, and development. The original Uppsala model of internationalization elaborated in the 1970s is later revised by the same authors, Johanson and Vahlne (2009), due to the changes in the IB scenario and dynamics. In their updated model, they emphasize the relevance of the network that a firm is able to set up in its national and international environment. In this new version, they attribute a crucial role to the company networks, consistently with the fundamentals of international entrepreneurship, based on the recognition of business opportunities by international entrepreneurs and the network approach (McDougall and Oviatt 2005).

The definition of psychic distance by Johanson and Vahlne (1977) includes the psychic and the cultural aspect. Hofstede (1980) and later Kogut and Singh (1988) elaborate a classification of cultural distances in terms of cross-country distance that is used as a measurement scale to capture national differences (Hennart and Larimo 1998). However, psychic distance studies are about the existing perceived differences between home and host country, and individual perceptions of differences come into issue (Child et al. 2009). While studies about cultural differences are mainly conducted at country level and do not look at what individuals perceive, they mainly look "outside" of the individual. The construct of cultural distance is generally analyzed at three main levels: country, firm, and individual (Hofstede 1980; Forsgren 2002; Cheng 2006; Jiang 2006; Brewer and Venaik 2011; Ambos and Håkanson 2014). The country level focuses on the values and behavior of the society as a whole; the firm level is based on certain business practices; and the individual level concerns the individuals' perceptions of distance. Nevertheless, Hofstede's and Kogut and Singh's (1988) composite indices do not capture the complexity of differences between the home and host country. Specifically, they neglect the role of societal institutions in disseminating and arbitrating cultural and social cues (Xu and Shenkar 2002). According to Shenkar (2001), the cultural distance indices do not apply to FDI as they fail to yield consistent empirical evidence and include some hidden assumptions which are named "illusions," such as the illusions of homogeneity and symmetry. The illusion of homogeneity concept takes for granted the fact that there is no difference of values in the same country, that is intra-country level. According to the illusion of symmetry, the distance perceived from country A toward country B can be different than the one perceived from country B toward A.

The distance issue is strongly related to two critical steps in the FDI process: host country selection and foreign entry strategy (Xu and Shenkar 2002). The concept of distance in internationalization is not only examined under several perspectives and perceptions but also taking into account a variety of dimensions and features, for instance, geographical (Fung et al. 2005; Zihui et al. 2008, Child et al. 2009) and institutional distance, such as the degree of corruption (Chantasasawat et al. 2010). Next to this, a cultural viewpoint (Cheng 2006) in terms of ties (Chen and Chen 1998) or cultural and ethnical proximity (Parmentola 2011) is also taken into account.

2.2 Psychic Distance and Culture Perceptions in the OLI Paradigm

Among other factors, cultural distance and psychic distance, in particular, are mentioned in the OLI eclectic paradigm (Dunning 1980) as key drivers in the FDI decisions since they pertain to location and internationalization choices. Accordingly, FDI is determined by three types of advantages: ownership, location, and internationalization (thus, OLI). The ownership advantage arises from the firm's size and access to markets and resources, and the ability to coordinate complementary activities (e.g., manufacturing and distribution) and to exploit differences between countries. The distance issue may arise from differences in the form of culture (Hong and Chen 2001; Brouthers et al. 1996a, b; Jiang 2006), bureaucratic procedures (Spigarelli 2010), or country characteristics (Zihui 2008). Those differences do not always guarantee the success of the choice. However, in the case of China, their absence and the ignorance of the Chinese culture (e.g., the importance of guanxi) may lead to failure (Jiang 2006).

The firm specific advantage is usually intangible and can be transferred within the MNE at low cost. Compared to a local competitor, a MNE operating a plant in a foreign country faces additional costs that could include legal, institutional, cultural, and language diversities. Location advantages of different countries are crucial to determine which will become a company's host country. Such advantages include differences in country's natural endowments, transportation costs, macroeconomic stability, cultural factors, and government regulation. According to this model, psychic distance belongs to the country specific advantage group since it is part of the social and cultural features, together with language, cultural diversities, general attitudes toward foreigners, and the overall position toward free enterprise (Brouthers et al. 1996a, b). This subgroup goes along with economic and political advantages (Hong and Chen 2001; Jiang 2006).

While quantities and qualities of the production factors, transportation and telecommunication costs, and scope and size of the market belong to the economic advantages and common and specific government policies that influence inward FDI flows, intra-firm trade belongs to the political advantages (Fung et al. 2005). Dunning (1997) shows that in determining FDI locations, transaction, and coordination cost variables, such as interpersonal relations, information asymmetries, language and culture are more important than production-related variables. Despite the fact that differences are not always translated into a success factor (Jiang 2006), it is argued that the internationalization incentives arise from exploiting imperfections in external markets. They entail reduction in uncertainty and transaction costs to generate knowledge more efficiently than state-generated imperfections, for instance, tariffs, foreign exchange controls, and subsidies. An integrated view of these advantages and the interaction with one another produce the final decision on FDI location (Jajri 2009).

2.3 OLI's Evolution to OLMA and Institutional Theory Traits

Dunning's OLI theory (Dunning 1980, etc.) provides a framework for many researchers who examine the interaction between various determinants of IB activities and entry modes (Brouthers et al. 1996a, b, 1999; Tse et al. 1997). Brouthers et al. (1999) further suggest that this paradigm might be used as a normative model. It provides a balanced overarching framework that helps to identify the determinants of the cross-border expansion strategy, especially FDI (Dunning et al. 2007). Dunning (2000) reconfigures the OLI paradigm to include asset FDI and MNEs activity. The OLI framework has been explained in detail in most FDI literature (Ramasamy 2003) since it is able to provide a theory for FDI activities under normal conditions. Nevertheless, Dunning (1993) himself admits that the paradigm is a general framework to determine the extent and the patterns of both foreign-owned production and domestic production rather than a theory of MNE or of FDI. This goes along with Hosseini's study (2005), since he proposes an alternative perspective to "read" the FDI decisions by applying a behaviorally based model (Heiner 1985) because it seems to reflect the international reality, made up of not only economic factors, but also political and cultural ones. A behavioral economics approach would enable to view a multinational firm as a complex organization in which all the three aspects intertwine and play a significant role.

Guisinger (2001) elaborates an evolved eclectic paradigm by replacing the "I" factor, which stands for "*internalization,*" with "M" for the "entry mode," shedding light on the distinction between factors affecting different modes of entry in various countries. The model foresees the adaptation of the firm's operations to the IB environment building on institutional theory; hence, OLMA stands for ownership, location, entry mode, and adaptation. Accordingly, there is a difference between foreign and domestic components of the environment. Within this context, North (2005) divides the environment into organizations and institutions. He names the institutions "geovalent component." In particular, he refers to institutional rules, regulations, cultures, and exchange rates as well as other elements that are geographically bound and in certain cases, but not always, follow national boundaries. It is about environmental forces that affect the firm but are not themselves organizations. This component is meaningful for adaptation and accommodation approaches to the IB environment (Guisinger 2001), consistently with the role that psychic distance plays in the international scenario. Next to the geovalent component, the author divides the environment in organizations, named "interactors."

As far as institutions are concerned, the literature seems to embed them into distance dimensions, essential in IB and international management research areas (Rottig and Reus 2009). Institutional distance measures have been much under the attention of and criticized by international scholars (Kogut and Singh 1988; Shenkar 2001) for neglecting such assumptions as intra-country differences and intra-country heterogeneity of cultures. Evidence is large and not limited to MNEs (Kostova 1999; Xu and Shenkar 2002), and recent streams of research increasingly consider their vital impact on firms, their performance, and their patterns of expansion and strategies.

When operating in distant environments that differ from the source context, institutional distance is considered as one of the key drivers of the liability of foreignness that firms need to face (Gehmawat 2001; Zaheer 1995). The literature identifies three main institutional pillars—regulative, normative, and cognitive (Kostova 1999)—that are strictly related to perceptions and subjective evaluation of the foreign environment. Apart from the regulative pillar regarding the existing laws and rules in certain contexts, the normative and the cognitive dimensions are particularly relevant to the present research. The normative dimension is about individuals' values and norms, and it is related to the social life, while the cognitive dimension concerns categories at cognitive level shared by people in a particular country (Kostova 1999), and it is about how people categorize their perceived reality. In the conceptual-theoretical work on institutional distance, both normative and cognitive distance are not always considered explicitly, but embedded in the cultural dimension (Kogut and Singh 1988). This chapter focuses on the cognition rather than the normative elements. Building on Child et al.'s (2009) study, psychic distance is defined as the existing perceived distance between home and host countries in terms of the following characteristics: factual (Johanson and Wiedersheim-Paul 1975; Johanson and Vahlne 1977), cognitive (Evans et al. 2000), and perceptual (Stöttinger and Schlegelmilch 2000).

2.4 OLI's Integration with LLL Theory and Emerging Countries MNEs Internationalization

Moving on the developments of the OLI paradigm, Mathews (2006) proposes the so-called linkage, leverage, and learning (LLL) framework, which has been defined as a complement to Dunning's (1993) eclectic paradigm. This contribution acknowledges that emerging countries MNEs may be willing to invest in more advanced countries to access or augment their resources rather than to exploit their ownership advantage. Linkages with foreign firms would foster the access to the resources they lack internally; subsequently, leverage would refer to how they can access the potential resources. The interaction between linkages and leverage may be conducive to learning related to the final outcome based on the opportunity to better understand how to operate internally and to allow firms to be competitive in the global markets.

In the context of emerging economies, MNEs seem not to follow the traditional patterns of development. The OLI paradigm could not explain these difficult patterns. In other words, it does not appear to explain the outreach toward international markets (Dunning 1993; Hosseini 2005). MNEs from emerging economies internationalize not because of their current advantages on a global scale, but to achieve competitive advantages (e.g., Spigarelli 2010). The exploitation of opportunities, thanks to their positions as late entrants to the market, seems to be a key factor in global success. This goes along with the fundamentals of international entrepreneurship proposed by McDougall and Oviatt (2005). Thus, Spigarelli (2010) proposes that a new ad hoc theory is needed to interpret the flows of international investment following the recent phases of expansion, especially regarding the Chinese case. Other scholars argue that countries experiencing a rapid development (e.g., China) are giving rise to new models of internationalization, therefore the need to revise and consolidate the theoretical frameworks that the current literature offers (Aulakh 2007).

3 Methodology

The criteria used to find relevant journal articles are based on the search cues "foreign direct investment*," "determinant*," "China" in the "Abstract," and in the following databases: *Business Source Premier*, *EconLit*, *Regional Business News* accessed through *EBSCOhost* and *ABI/INFORM*. This searching procedure delivered 35 results.

Regarding the criteria of inclusion and exclusion, among the 35 journal articles, only documents focused on China and FDI were considered relevant. Four articles were "partly relevant" to this research since they deal with China, but focus on other issues: the "China effect" (Chantasasawat et al. 2004, 2010), the determinants of disparities in inward FDI in China (Zheng 2011), and the Japanese investment in Asian host countries in general (Langhammer 1991). Other six articles were "not relevant" since they explore the regional per capita income distribution in China (Villaverde and Maza 2012), the determinants of city growth in China (Anderson and Ge 2004), the firm specific effects on location decision of FDI in China (Hong 2007), the influence of FDI on the growth of Malaysia (Jairi 2009), the global city-regions in China (Zhao and Zhang 2007), patterns and determinants of FDI in Malaysia from a comparative Southeast Asian perspective (Athukorala and Waglé 2011), and the diffusion and absorption of technological knowledge (Liao et al. 2012). Finally, one of the articles is about FDI and Russia (Iwasaki and Suganuma 2005). These studies resulted from the searching procedure because they include the above-mentioned keywords searched in the abstract but are not purposeful for the research questions of this systematic literature review: Is psychic distance a key FDI determinant in the Chinese marketplace and to what extent?[5]

The above-mentioned papers are not relevant to the Chinese case, but they are useful to analyze whether psychic distance is a relevant object of studies among FDI determinants, regardless of the involvement of the Chinese marketplace.

Next to the documents obtained from the aforementioned databases, the snowballing technique (Jalali and Wohlin 2012) was adopted on the basis of the relevant citations appearing in the 35 results. This additional searching procedure produced 82 documents resulted in a total of 117. The following sections analyze and discuss the key findings.

4 Analysis

Evidence shows a small number of studies have used psychic distance as FDI determinants in the Chinese case. Specifically, 17 papers cover the "psychic distance" topic. However, only 6 out of 17 papers focus on FDI (see Table 2).

The study by Chen and Chen (1998) refers to psychological closeness and proximity rather than psychic distance. In this chapter, China and Taiwan are examined. Concerning investors, China is psychologically close to Taiwan in terms of culture and communication, although

Table 2 Studies on PD, China, India, Japan, Taiwan, Australia, and FDI determinants

Authors	Year of publication	Academic journal
Chen, H., Chen, T.-J.	1998	Journal of International Business Studies
Forsgren, M.	2002	International Business Review
Zihui, M., Ruilong Y., Zhang, Y	2008	Economic Papers
Buckley, P.J., Cross, A.R., Horn, S.A.	2012	Business History
Hashim, F.	2012	Review of Business & Finance Studies
Amighini, A.A., Rabellotti, R. Sanfilippo, M.	2013	China Economic Review

they are distant in terms of political and economic systems. As first, the authors refer to the perception of location familiarity that measures investors' prior market experience in the host country in the form of exporting or licensing. Second, they refer to the investors' perceived distance of the host country in the form of affinities and similarities of culture, political system, economic conditions, and communication. They confirm Grosse and Trevino's (1996) findings on the relevance of cultural and geographical distances, which discourage FDI decisions. The study by Forsgren (2002) (Table 2) does consider psychic distance. This is a critical review of the Uppsala model of internationalization, adding a controversial point. The author argues that psychic distance is basically a concept regarding the national level, while foreign investment is a phenomenon involving the management level. Ambos and Håkanson (2014) highlight the importance of the level of analysis. They point out that psychic distance should be analyzed at firm and individual levels. However, the national level should run parallel to them. This leads to an integrated analysis of the perceptions that enables to capture the different nuances of the construct at all the three levels—national, firm, and personal.

In the third study, the Asian investors are compared with the Australians. Zihui et al. (2008) refer to the fact that Asian investors in China differ greatly from Australia in economic structure, per capita income, cultural ties with, and geographical proximity to, China. Generally speaking, the literature considers these features as ingredients of the psychic distance construct. The authors highlight that it is therefore worth investigating whether the determinants of Australian FDI conform to the general pattern of inward FDI in China. Not only objectively measurable determinants, but also qualitative ones are important. They all contribute to the promotion of Australian FDI in China in terms of policy design.

The authors of the fourth paper (Buckley et al. 2012) consider the "distance" issue being part of FDI determinants. However, their work does not focus on the Chinese marketplace. Their case about Japan and India shows that along with geographical distance and psychic distance, risk averseness may be also responsible for the hesitant behavior of Japanese firms toward India. Results show that Japanese managers keep seeing India as psychically distant from Japan. Nevertheless, in this specific case, it is the institutional factor (Kostova 1999; Rottig and Reus 2009) that is the crucial determinant in Indo-Japanese economic relations rather than the notion of psychic distance due to India's import substitution policy. This is to demonstrate how FDI determinants depend on the country pairs that are examined and their institutional, environmental, and behavioral characteristics. In support of this, Mathews (2006) argues that globalization includes a number of processes and phenomena next to the integration of financial systems, trade liberalization, deregulation, and market opening. This is an orientation toward a cultural, economic, and social homogeneity. Nevertheless, this is not the case if specific country pairs of different continents are taken into account, such as China and Italy. Therefore, we can refer to globalization in terms of generalization, but if specific case studies are considered, this generalization is no longer applicable due to a wide range of differences. Under this perspective, psychic distance and cultural distance are called upon: It is exactly here where the countries involved in the comparison collide or unify or even complement themselves (Mathews 2006).

The fifth work on Malaysian FDI to China (Hashim 2012) shows that psychic distance plays a pivotal role in foreign expansion strategies. The author supports the applicability of the Uppsala incremental process of internationalization and the positive role played by the awareness of psychic distance perception, which reduces uncertainties and risks of failure in foreign markets. The sixth and last chapters (Amighini et al. 2013) also support Hashim's study (2012) by stating that psychic distance and the issue of psychically distant market perceptions do matter. The authors emphasize the role of the international relations with overseas Chinese for Chinese companies since they are considered a crucial source of information and location attraction factors.

According to the theoretical background which provides with an overview of the main theories applicable in FDI decisions, psychic distance is a key element of the Uppsala internationalization model (Johanson and Vahlne 1977, 2009). The following articles support this theory (see Table 3).

Table 3 Articles regarding Asia supporting the concept of PD according to the Uppsala scholars

Authors	Year of publication	Academic journal
Walters, P.G.P.	1996	International Journal of Information Management
Dunning, J.H.	2000	International Business Review
Xu, D., Shenkar, O.	2002	Academy of Management Review
Stoian, C., Filippaios, F.	2008	International Business Review
Luo, Y., Shenkar, O.	2011	Journal of International Management
Luiz, J.M., Ruplal, M.	2013	Emerging Markets Finance and Trade
Ambos, B., Håkanson, L.	2014	Journal of International Management

e.g., Johanson and Vahlne (1977, 2009)

An exceptional investigation on psychic distance by O'Grady and Lane (1996) highlights the fact that perceptions of familiarity and similarity across geographically close countries or similar countries, for example English-speaking countries, is not always a synonym of closeness (Henderson 2005). For instance, geographically close home and host countries do not necessarily share the same business practices. Overconfidence attributed to the similarity of languages or to cultural aspects may lead to misperceptions and thereby to a negative impact on the business communication processes as well as personal relationships. This is defined as "psychic distance paradox" (O'Grady and Lane 1996).

Although the issue of non-physical distance does not appear consistently among the main FDI determinants, many IB and international management scholars have been deeply exploring the topic and are aware of the subjective aspect of the concept. Rather than focusing on the second word of the concepts "psychic distance" and "cultural distance" (thus, "distance"), a deeper analysis of the relationship between the "psychic" and "cultural" terms may be necessary. For example, Spigarelli (2010), Al-Huda and Karim (2012) confirm their interest in the two strongly related constructs. Spigarelli (2010) refers to "psychological distances" and relates it to "cultural affinity." While Al-Huda and Karim (2012) argue that the psychic distance concept includes the cultural factor next to the geographical, legal, and linguistic variables, both "distances" play a relevant role in the IB literature.

5 Discussion

The results analyzed in this systematic literature review show how psychic distance has its valuable space in the IB literature but has not been taken into account as much as other economic and quantifiable FDI determinants. The previous sections confirm two directions: on the one hand, the influence of psychic distance perceptions and of cultural and political features in the decision-making process; on the other hand, the difficulty to quantify and measure such variables in IB. As a matter of fact, scholars have tried to study and measure those subjective variables. Hofstede's (1980) dimensions of culture and other indices elaborated in subsequent studies over the years are some examples. Kogut and Singh's (1988) composite index is based on Hofstede's work. Drogendijk and Slangen (2006) support the validity of the cultural distance indices proposed by Hofstede (1980) and later by Schwartz in 1994, who elaborated another composite index based on their prior work. According to Drogendijk and Slangen (2006), it is premature to dismiss these indices and consider them as outdated or inaccurate.

5.1 The Case of China: Relevant Findings

Recently, China has been one of the most studied cases by international scholars (Parmentola 2011; Villaverde and Maza 2012). However, only 25 IB journal articles resulting from the search procedures illustrated above cover the Chinese marketplace, FDI determinants and psychic distance altogether. Shedding light on the issue of FDI direction, scholars identify in-, out-, and intra-country flows. Three out of 25 articles are about outbound FDI. This shows that China not only is one of the largest recipients of FDI but has been also playing an active role worldwide as far as outbound FDI is concerned (Spigarelli 2010; UNCTAD 2014). Generally speaking, developed economies expect a gradual recovery of FDI in the current year, and it can be assumed that this phenomenon will be deeper investigated by scholars from now onward, especially covering the Chinese marketplace. This forecast is supported by the role played by cultural or historical ties of Chinese residents with other Chinese abroad or overseas Chinese that may be crucial resources in explaining outward-trends of FDI. Thanks to these relations and the presence of Chinese in the rest of the world, the ability to exploit ties within the same ethnic networks worldwide is proven to be fundamental. Spigarelli (2010) confirms that "cultural affinity goes along with psychological closeness perceptions." This intertwines with the geographical viewpoint. For example, Chinese investments in Italy are strongly related to the local presence of Chinese residents (e.g., the city of Prato in Tuscany).

An increasing knowledge of foreign markets by multinational firms is gained through experience from the interaction between factors captured by the concept of psychic distance, which includes not only cultural, linguistic, and legal elements, but also the geographical differences and distance between two business locations (Al-Huda and Karim 2012). Furthermore, legal, normative, and cognitive aspects which draw from institutional theories are also considered (Scott 1995; Kostova 1999; Rottig and Reus 2009).

According to Amighini et al. (2013), "cross-border" *guanxi* among the Chinese diaspora seems to be a relevant attraction factor in location decisions. Guanxi can be defined as "relational entities and their relationships, as social practices of building and using personal relationships to get through life and work, as a strategy for organizations to gain competitive advantage and as a mechanism of contracting and transactions" (Chen et al. 2013: 169). In other words, exploitation of relational assets reduces psychic distance with institutionally different countries. For this reason, local networks of overseas Chinese are considered a crucial source of information—and trustworthiness—for Chinese companies in a psychically distant market. This is likely to affect the success or the failure of the investment or business. Entrepreneurship is a dynamic activity; between 2004 and 2007, the presence of the Chinese entrepreneurs increased by 45%. Scholars refer to "ethnic specialization," meaning a concentration of Chinese entrepreneurs, in specific business segments and about "industry ethnicization," that is the trend of this ethnic group to saturate business initiatives of initial establishment. Next to this, they tend to favor areas that offer a wide range of peculiar skills.

The impact of transnational ties in the realm of FDI is crucial, as the author illustrates a striking example of how the presence of potential political and military public interests may impede international integration and transactions (Spigarelli 2010). Chen et al. (2004) also emphasize the role of cultural background and affinity in Chinese IB relationships. In least institutionalized markets such as Southeast Asia, initial network connections with related firms and ethnic links to Chinese diaspora play an important role in facilitating and fostering FDI.

5.2 "Affinity" in Cultural, Background, and Institutional Features

Non-economic factors are argued to affect both the amount and direction of investment flows (e.g., bureaucratization of authorization procedures) which might be related to institutional features. The focus on intangible assets, such as government policies, can be reflected in institutional distance, since government and companies are connected in interventions and reforms. Therefore, this affects managerial culture and risk perceptions (Spigarelli 2010). As far as bureaucratic difficulties are concerned, a certain degree of symmetry can be found, and this should be further examined. Such issues affect the decision making of an investment in a specific country, including symmetric weaknesses encountered mutually by country A toward country B and by country B toward A. This is consistent with what the Uppsala School predicts in considering historical, economic, and cultural ties between the home and host economy at the initial stage of the internationalization process (Johanson and Vahlne 1977). And at a later stage, countries with low psychic distance are taken into account due to the capitalization of experience after moving into other more distant economies (Stoian and Filoppaios 2008). Besides, the reexamination of the Uppsala model by Johanson and Vahlne (2009) confirms that psychic distance insists to be important in the current global scenario though weaker. A company network may transcend the geographical boundaries and internationalize through the exploitation of business network opportunities, drawing the conclusion that the selection criterion for mining FDI depends on minimization of the distance between the home country and the host country (Luiz and Ruplal 2013).

6 Conclusion

The present study shows how psychic distance as a determinant of Chinese FDI flows is under-investigated in the IB literature. However, scholars have worked on "distance" topics over the years since "psychic distance" first appeared in the 1950s. The concept was examined under various perspectives by considering a variety of features and "dimensions," drawing from the extant theories which propose how to define and operationalize the concept. The reasons may lie in the need for IB research to quantify variables in empirical studies by including psychic distance perceptions at different levels of analysis: individual, firm/group, industry, and country level.

As about the models used to isolate the psychic distance determinant, no consistent material appeared in the methodology parts of the analyzed works. The main findings illustrated in this research can be considered as a premise to confirm the need for further research on psychic distance, FDI flows, and FDI determinants related to the Chinese marketplace. China and its specific host countries can be the business settings to investigate psychic distance on a specific level of analysis.

China is now widening its presence abroad, not only in the Eastern world regions but also in the psychically distant countries of the "West." This means that Chinese investors have to carry out an attentive examination of FDI determinants concerning distance issues (e.g., psychic, cultural, institutional, and geographical distance) along with the mere economic and objectively measurable factors traditionally taken into account.

Most of the studies so far have studied the relationships between the Western and Eastern economies considering China as a passive actor.

Now an inversion of trend in research is necessary to predict and to analyze its impact on other actors and markets around the world.

As a work-in-progress study within an EU project regarding partnership opportunities between Europe and China, the final results of this research are expected to come in 2016. A questionnaire covering not only economic aspects but also differences in the regulatory system, language, culture, and perceptions is currently being submitted to a wide range of companies operating in the green sector and environmental industry in China and Europe.[6] Two future lines of research can follow up this study. First, the elaboration of a new theoretical framework with the purpose to explain the role of "differences" between Europe and China is necessary. Second, individual perceptions of "distance" between a certain country and China as a home or host country could also be examined. In this case, existing psychic distance operationalization can be applied in a specific business setting. The analysis could be conducted at firm or industry level by taking into account managers' perceptions of psychic distance along each of its components (e.g., cultural and legal aspects). A new framework or existing psychic distance models can be tested within the EU project embracing markets in China and Europe, thanks to the data collected through the survey addressed to the European firms investing in China and the Chinese firms investing in Europe.

Notes

1. "This project is funded by the European Union under the Marie Curie Action's IRSES." 2) "This publication does not necessarily reflect the opinion of the EU" [When relevant]. The research leading to these results has received funding from the People Programme (Marie Curie Actions) of the European Union's Seventh Framework Programme FP7/2007-2013/under REA grant agreement no 318908.
2. Hymer's study is about the criticism of the neoclassical application of the portfolio flows theory. He transported the theory of foreign direct investment out of the neoclassical international theories of trade and finance and into industrial organization, the study of market imperfections.

3. However, according to some scholars, FDI may crowd out local companies and has negative effects on economic development (Vintila 2010).
4. Its evolution from 1958 to 2000 is illustrated in detail by Ferreira et al. (2011).
5. Another pertinent question would be how scholars identify and isolate the variable in their models of analysis, but there are not consistent results about this as the most rigorous models are related to other variables, which are quantitatively measured (Zihui et al. 2008; Sanfilippo 2010; Villaverde and Maza 2012).
6. The questionnaire is available in two versions in order to near both Chinese and European respondents: The Chinese version is addressed to the Chinese investors in Europe and the English version to the European firms investing in China.

References

Al-Huda, N., & Karim, A. (2012). Factors affecting foreign direct investment in Malaysia's manufacturing sector: An analysis across states. *The Singapore Economic Review, 57*(4), 1–14.

Ambos, B., & Håkanson, L. (2014). The concept of distance in international management research. *Journal of International Management, 20*(1), 1–7.

Amighini, A. A., Rabellotti, R., & Sanfilippo, M. (2013). Do Chinese state-owned and private enterprises differ in their internationalization strategies? *China Economic Review, 27,* 312–325.

Anderson, G., & Ge, Y. (2004). Do economic reforms accelerate urban growth? The case of China. *Urban Studies, 41*(11), 2197–2210.

Athukorala, P. C., & Waglé, S. (2011). Foreign direct investment in Southeast Asia: Is Malaysia falling behind? *ASEAN Economic Bulletin, 28*(2), 115–133.

Aulakh, P. S. (2007). Emerging multinationals from developing economies: Motivations, paths and performance. *Journal of International Management, 13*(3), 235–402.

Bartels, F. L., Napolitano, F., & Tissi, N. E. (2014). FDI in Sub-Saharan Africa: A longitudinal perspective on location-specific factors (2003–2010). *International Business Review, 23,* 516–529.

Beckerman, W. (1956). Distance and the pattern of intra-European trade. *The Review of Economics and Statistics, 38*(31), 31–40.

Brewer, P., & Venaik, S. (2011). Individualism–collectivism in Hofstede and GLOBE. *Journal of International Business Studies, 42*(3), 436–445.
Brouthers, K. D., Brouthers, L. E., & Werner, S. (1996a). Dunning's eclectic paradigm theory and the small firm: The impact of ownership and local advantages on the choice of entry modes in the computer software industry. *International Business Review, 5*(4), 337–394.
Brouthers, K. D., Brouthers, L. E., & Werner, S. (1996b). Is Dunning's eclectic framework descriptive or normative? *Journal of International Business Studies, 30*(4), 831–844.
Brouthers, L. E., Brouthers, K. D., & Werner, S. (1999). Is Dunning's eclectic framework descriptive or normative? *Journal of International Business Studies, 30*(4), 831–844.
Buckley, P. J., Cross, A. R., & Horn, S. A. (2012). Japanese foreign direct investment in India: An institutional theory approach. *Business History, 54*(5), 657–688.
Buckley, P.J., & Casson, M.C. (1976). *The future of the multinational enterprise.* London: Homes & Meier.
Chakrabarti, A. (2001). The determinants of foreign direct investments: Sensitivity analyses of cross-country regressions. *Kyklos, 54*(1), 89–114.
Chantasasawat, B., Fung, K. C., Iizaka, H., & Siu, A. (2004). The giant sucking sound: Is China diverting foreign direct investment from other Asian economies? *Asian Economic Papers, 3*(3), 122–140.
Chantasasawat, B., Fung, K. C., Iizaka, H., & Siu, A. (2010). FDI flows to Latin America, East and Southeast Asia, and China: Substitute or complements? *Review of Development Economics, 14*(3), 533–546.
Chen, H., & Chen, T.-J. (1998). Network linkages and location choice in foreign direct investment. *Journal of International Business Studies, 29*(3), 445–467.
Chen, C. C., Chen, X.-P., & Huang, S. (2013). Chinese *guanxi*: An integrative review and new directions for future research. *Management and Organization Review, 9*(1), 167–207.
Chen, T.-J., Chen, H., & Ku, Y.-H. (2004). Foreign direct investment and local linkages. *Journal of International Business Studies, 35*, 320–333.
Cheng, Y.-M. (2006). Determinants of FDI mode choice: Acquisition, brownfield, and greenfield entry in foreign markets. *Canadian Journal of Administrative Sciences Review, 23*(3), 202–220.

Cheng, L. K., & Kwan, Y. K. (2000). What are the determinants of the location of foreign direct investment? The Chinese experience. *Journal of International Economics, 51,* 379–400.

Child, J., Rodrigues, S. B., & Frynas, J. G. (2009). Psychic distance, its impact and coping modes: Interpretations of SMEs decision-makers. *Management International Review, 49*(2), 199–224.

Coase, R. H. (1937). The nature of the firm. *Economica. New Series, 4*(16), 386–405.

Coughlin, C. C., & Segev, E. (2000). Foreign direct investment in China: A spatial econometric study. *The World Economy, 3*(1), 1–23.

Cushman, D. O. (1985). Real exchange rate risk, expectations and the level of direct investment. *Review of Economics and Statistics, 67*(2), 297–308.

Dow, D., & Karunaratna, A. (2006). Developing a multidimensional instrument to measure psychic distance stimuli. *Journal of International Business Studies, 37*(5), 578–602.

Drogendijk, R., & Slangen, A. (2006). Hofstede, Schwartz, or managerial perceptions? The effects of different cultural distance measures on establishment mode choices by multinational enterprises. *International Business Review, 15,* 361–380.

Dunning, J. H. (1980). Toward an eclectic theory of international production: Some empirical tests. *Journal of International Business Studies, 11*(1), 9–31.

Dunning, J. H. (1993). *Multinational enterprises and the global economy.* Harlow: Addison-Wesley.

Dunning, J. H. (2000). The eclectic paradigm as an envelope for economic and business theories of MNE activity. *International Business Review, 9,* 163–190.

Dunning, J. H. (2009). Location and the multinational enterprise: John Dunning's thoughts on receiving the journal of international business studies 2008 decade award. *Journal of International Business Studies, 40,* 20–34.

Dunning, J. H., & Bansal, S. (1997). The cultural sensitivity of the eclectic paradigm. *Multinational Business Review, 5*(1), 1–16.

Dunning, J. H., Pak, Y. S., & Beldona, S. (2007). Foreign ownership strategies of UK and US international franchisors: An exploratory application of Dunning's envelope paradigm. *International Business Review, 16,* 531–548.

Evans, J., Treadgold, A., & Mavondo, F. (2000). Explaining export development through psychic distance. *International Marketing Review, 17*(2), 164–169.

Ferreira, M. P., Pinto, C. F., Serra, F. A. R., & Gaspar, L. F. (2011). John Dunning's influence in international business/strategy research: A bibliometric study in the strategic management journal. *Journal of Strategic Management Education, 7*(2), 77–99.

Forsgren, M. (2002). The concept of learning in the Uppsala internationalization process model: A critical review. *International Business Review, 11,*(3) 257–277.

Fung, K. C., Garcia-Herrero, A., Iizaka, H., & Siu, A. (2005). Hard or soft? Institutional reforms and infrastructure spending as determinants of foreign direct investment in China. *The Japanese Economic Review, 56*(4), 408–416.

Ghemawat, P. (2001). Distance still matters. *Harvard Business Review, 79*(8), 137–147.

Gomez-Mejia, L., & Polick, L. (1997). Cultural diversity and the performance of multinational firms. *Journal of International Business Studies, 28*(2), 309–335.

Grosse, R., & Trevino, L. J. (1996). Foreign direct investment in the United States: An analysis by country of origin. *Journal of International Business Studies, 27*(1), 139–155.

Gruber, W. H., & Vernon, R. (1970). The technology factor in a world trade matrix. In R. Vernon (Ed.), *The Technology Factor in International Trade* (pp. 233–272). New York: Columbia University Press for National Bureau of Economic Research.

Guisinger, S. (2001). From OLI to OLMA: Incorporating higher levels of environmental and structural complexity into the eclectic paradigm. *International Journal of the Economics of Business, 8*(2), 257–272.

Hashim, F. (2012). Outward internationalization and FDI: Motives for Malaysian MNEs moving into China. *Review of Business and Finance Studies, 3*(2), 89–102.

Heiner, R. (1985). Origins of predictive behavior: Further modeling applications. *American Economics Review, 75*(2), 391–396.

Hennart, J. F. (1982). *A theory of multinational enterprise.* Ann Arbor: University of Michigan.

Hennart, J. F., & Larimo, J. (1998). The impact of culture on the strategy of multinational enterprises: Does national origin affect ownership decisions? *Journal of International Business Studies, 29,* 515–538.

Henderson, J. K. (2005). Language diversity in international management teams. *International Studies of Management and Organization, 35*(1), 66–82.

Hofstede, G. (1980). *Culture's consequences: International differences in work-related values*. Beverly Hills, CA: Sage.
Hong, J. (2007). Firm-specific effects on location decisions of foreign direct investment in China's logistics industry. *Regional Studies, 41*(5), 673–683.
Hong, M., & Chen, L. S. (2001). Quantitative and dynamic analysis of the OLI variables determining FDI in China. *Review of Urban & Regional Development Studies, 13*(2), 163–172.
Hosseini, H. (2005). An economic theory of FDI: A behavioural economics and historical approach. *The Journal of Socio-Economics, 34,* 528–541.
Hymer, S. H. (1960). *The international operation of national firms: A study of direct investment.* M.I.T Ph.D. dissertation, Published by M.I.T. Press in 1976.
Iwasaki, I., & Suganuma, K. (2005). Regional distribution of foreign direct investment in Russia. *Post-Communist Economies, 17*(2), 153–172.
Jalali, S., & Wohlin, C. (2012). Systematic literature studies: Database searches vs. Backward snowballing. In *International Conference on Empirical Software Engineering and Measurement, ESEM'12,* September 19–20, 2012, Lund, Sweden. http://www.wohlin.eu/esem12a.pdf. Accessed Apr 2017.
Jajri, I. (2009). Foreign direct investment and economic growth: Cointegration techniques. *The IUP Journal of Managerial Economics, 3*(4), 7–18.
Jiang, F. (2006). The determinants of the effectiveness of foreign direct investment in China: An empirical study of joint and sole ventures. *International Journal of Management, 23*(4), 891–908.
Johanson, J., & Vahlne, E. (1977). The internationalization process of the firm: A model of knowledge development and increasing foreign market commitments. *Journal of International Business Studies, 8,* 23–32.
Johanson, J., & Vahlne, E. (2009). The Uppsala internationalization process model revisited: From liability of foreignness to liability of outsidership. *Journal of International Business Studies, 40*(9), 1411–1431.
Johanson, J., & Wiedersheim-Paul, F. (1975). The internationalization of the firm—four Swedish cases. *Journal of Management Studies, 12*(3), 305–323.
Kogut, B., & Singh, H. (1988). The effect of national culture on the choice of entry mode. *Journal of International Business Studies, 19,* 411–432.
Kostova, T. (1999). Transnational transfer of strategic organizational practices: A contextual perspective. *Academy of Management Review, 24*(2), 308–324.
Langhammer, R. J. (1991). Towards regional entities in Asia-Pacific. *ASEAN Economic Bulletin, 7*(3), 277–289.

Leamer, E. E. (1974). The commodity composition of international trade in manufactures: An empirical analysis. *Oxford Economic Papers, 26*(3), 350–374.

Lenartowicz, T., & Roth, K. (1999). A framework for culture assessment. *Journal of International Business Studies, 30*(4), 781–798.

Li, X., Hou, K., & Chan, M. W. L. (2008). An empirical study of foreign direct investment location in Eastern China. *The Chinese Economy, 41*(6), 75–98.

Liao, H., Liu, X., & Wang, C. (2012). Knowledge spillovers, absorptive capacity and total factor productivity in China's manufacturing firms. *International Review of Applied Economics, 26*(4), 533–547.

Linnemann, H. (1966). *An econometric study of international trade flows*. Amsterdam: North-Holland Publishing.

Luiz, J. M., & Ruplal, M. (2013). Foreign direct investment, institutional voids, and the internationalization of mining companies into Africa. *Emerging Markets Finance and Trade, 49*(4), 113–129.

Luo, Y., & Shenkar, O. (2011). Toward a perspective of cultural friction in international business. *Journal of International Management, 17*(1), 1–14.

Ma, Z., Yang, R., & Zhang, Y. (2008). Australia's direct investment in China: Trends and determinants. *Economic Papers, 27*(1), 70–86.

Markusen, J. (1995). The boundaries of multinational enterprises and the theory of international trade. *The Journal of Economic Perspectives, 9*(2), 169–191.

Mathews, J. A. (2006). Dragon multinationals: New players in 21st century globalization. *Asia Pacific Journal of Management, 23*(5), 5–27.

McDougall, P., & Oviatt, B. (2005). Defining international entrepreneurship and modeling the speed of internationalization. *Entrepreneurship Theory and Practice, 29*(5), 537–554.

North, D. C. (2005). *Understanding the process of economic change*. Princeton: Princeton University Press.

O'Grady, S., & Lane, H. (1996). The psychic distance paradox. *Journal of International Business Studies, 27*(2), 309–333.

Parmentola, A. (2011). The internationalization strategy of new Chinese multinationals: Determinants and evolution. *International Journal of Management, 28*(1), 369–386.

Ramasamy, B. (2003). FDI and uncertainty: The Malaysian case. *Journal of the Asia Pacific Economy, 8*(1), 85–101.

Roth, K., & O'Donnell, S. O. (1996). Foreign subsidiary compensation: An agency theory perspective. *Academy of Management Journal, 39*(3), 678–703.
Rottig, D., & Reus, T. H. (2009). Institutional distance, organizational legitimacy, and the performance of foreign acquisitions in the united states. In *Academy of Management Annual Meeting Proceedings* (pp. 1–6). Chicago: Academy of Management Proceedings.
Samuelson, P. (1948). International trade and the equalization of factor prices. *Economic Journal, 58,* 163–184.
Sanfilippo, M. (2010). Chinese FDI to Africa: What is the nexus with foreign economic cooperation? *African Development Review, 22*(1), 599–614.
Scott, W. R. (1995). *Institutions and organizations*. Thousand Oaks, CA: Sage.
Shenkar, O. (2001). Cultural distance revisited: Towards a more rigorous conceptualization and measurement of cultural differences. *Journal of International Business Studies, 32*(4), 519–535.
Spigarelli, F. (2009). Le multinazionali dei paesi emergenti: Gli investimenti cinesi in Italia (MNEs from emerging countries: Chinese investment in Italy. With English summary). *Economia Politica e Industriale, 36*(2), 131–159.
Spigarelli, F. (2010). Chinese investments in Italy: Is the wave arriving? *International Journal of Asian Business and Information Management, 1*(1), 54–76.
Stoian, C., & Filippaios, F. (2008). Dunning's eclectic paradigm: A holistic, yet context specific framework for analyzing the determinants of outward FDI evidence from international Greek investments. *International Business Review, 17,* 349–367.
Stöttinger, B., & Schlegelmilch, B. B. (2000). Psychic distance: A concept past its due date? *International Marketing Review, 17*(2), 169–173.
Tse, D. K., Pan, Y., & Au, K. Y. (1997). How MNCs choose entry modes and form alliances: The China experience. *Journal of International Business Studies, 28*(4), 779–805.
UNCTAD. (2014, January 28). *Global investment trends monitor*, No. 15, New York: United Nations.
Vernon, R. (1966). International investment and international trade in the product cycle. *Quarterly Journal of Economics, 80,* 190–207.
Villaverde, J., & Maza, A. (2012). Chinese per capita income distribution, 1992–2007: A regional perspective. *Asian Economic Journal, 26*(4), 313–331.

Vintila, D. (2010). Foreign direct investment theories: An overview of the main FDI theories. *European Journal of Interdisciplinary Studies, 2*(2), 104–110.

Walters, P. G. P. (1996). International market information infusion: Data acquisition behavior in Norwegian Exporters. *International Journal of Information Management, 16*(6), 437–444.

Wei, W., & Alon, I. (2010). Chinese outward direct investment: A study on macroeconomic determinants. *International Journal and Emerging Markets, 2*(4), 352–369.

Xiaojuan, J., Yingxin, W., & Laike, Y. (2004). A study of the gradual shift of foreign investment. *The Chinese Economy, 37*(5), 19–36.

Xu, D., & Shenkar, O. (2002). Institutional distance and the multinational enterprise. *Academy of Management Review, 27*(4), 608–618.

Zaheer, S. (1995). Overcoming the liability of foreignness. *Academy of Management Journal, 38*(2), 341–363.

Zhang, K. H. (2000). Why is U.S. direct investment in China so small? *Contemporary Economic Policy, 18*(1), 82–94.

Zhang, K. H. (2001a). China's inward FDI boom and the greater Chinese economy. *The Chinese Economy, 34*(1), 74–88.

Zhang, K. H. (2001b). What attracts foreign multinational corporations to China? *Contemporary Economic Policy, 19*(3), 336–346.

Zhao, S. X. B., & Zhang, L. (2007). Foreign direct investment and the formation of global city regions in China. *Regional Studies, 14*(7), 979–994.

Zheng, P. (2011). The determinants of disparities in inward FDI flows to the three macro-regions of China. *Post-Communist Economies, 23*(2), 257–270.

Zihui, M., Ruilong, Y., & Zhang, Y. (2008). Australia's direct investment in China: Trends and determinants. *Economic Papers, 27*, 70–86.

3

A Social Psychological Perspective on the Perceptions of Cultural Differences

Abstract Building on social psychology and international business literature, this chapter aims at raising managers' awareness on the opportunity to capitalize on cultural differences in cross-cultural business contexts. This work is based on survey data and interviews to European managers investing in China through FDI in the environmental industry. First, this work investigates managers' perceptions of culture within the multidimensional concept of psychic distance, which is a 12 dimension-based construct. Second, it explores what culture stands for our managers following our findings, which show the relevance of the cultural dimension over the others. Third, we propose and illustrate the *sociocognitive* value of an *intercultural laboratory* as a potential "structured business practice" addressed to those early-stage managers who are about to approach the firms' host country. The failing ethnocentric view is a common perspective adopted by managers in cross-cultural business settings. Therefore, the idea behind this chapter is to help international managers overcome this view and leverage on an

Authors are thankful to prof. Barbara Pojaghi and prof. Song Yang for their contribution to this chapter.

K. Vaccarini et al., *Cultural Distance in International Ventures*,
DOI 10.1007/978-3-319-62193-7_3

inter-individual and collective construction of knowledge, stimulated by the intercultural laboratory activities based on group work. The focus is on "opportunities"—rather than "distances"—generated by cultural diversities. Next to this, enhancing the "dialogue" between different cultures as well as different research areas is a key approach in cross-cultural business settings, not only for managers having different cultural backgrounds but also for scholars belonging to different discipline areas of research.

Keywords Social psychology · International business · Cultural differences · Cultural diversity · European investment to China · FDI Environmental industry · Managers' perceptions · Managers' awareness · Psychic distance dimensions · Cross-cultural business settings Sociocognity value · Intercultural laboratory

1 Introduction

Diversity may be highly beneficial rather than challenging or harmful under certain circumstances. This is the reason why in cross-cultural settings a specific training aimed at approaching diversity is necessary. Above all, this is particularly true in light of the growing intra-national heterogeneity within many countries in today's globalized world economy.

When dealing with home and host country, differences are a fact and cannot be ignored; therefore, individuals should create value out of them. Cultural diversity and differences lead to successful achievements and profitable investments in international business activities if they are approached and managed under a perspective, which is aimed at integration rather than homologation. Integration aims at reducing and decreasing cultural barriers within the home country and host country firm. While homologation can be described by a company investing abroad and "exporting" its business model in the host country firm with the aim of homologation rather than integration. What lies behind homologation is the univocal view of the world adopted by home country managers.

Drawing on survey data on managers' perceptions and their meaning of culture, this study draws scholars' attentions to the *sociocognitive* value of a specific training, which we call *group cultural laboratory* as a potential "structured business practice" to be adopted in cross-cultural business contexts. More specifically, this type of training in the form of a *laboratory* would be addressed to those early-step managers who are about approaching an international career in an international business setting. The purpose is to help them overcome the failing ethnocentric view, which is commonly adopted in international environments. Rather than aiming at homologation, cultural diversity offers opportunities for both home country and host country managers.

The fact that diversity fosters and stimulates working and research environments is confirmed by recent studies in social psychology. Heterogeneous environments foster creativity, as cognitive psychologists confirm (Cattaneo 2014). Generally speaking, the skill and the opportunity to change cultural references is a crucial ingredient in work and science, which is the creative activity of the human intellect *par excellance*. Working in heterogeneous environments, confronting with people who have different cultural backgrounds is not only a privilege but also an opportunity to widen one's own horizons (Cattaneo 2014). In support of this, Guterl (2014) argues that diversity is the heart of efficient research and innovation. Working groups benefit from diversity because people react differently to whom is different from them. Nevertheless, conducting research on cultural diversity presupposes challenges for scholars operating at international level due to the impediments to collect reliable data and on the availability of social and ethnic groups and categories (Cattaneo 2014).

First, this study contributes in overcoming this barriers by illustrating our research based on survey data collected in the fieldwork, thanks to the availability of our target, which is constituted by European managers representing European companies which operate in China in the environmental industry. Second, we would like to take the challenge of detecting and measuring managers' perceptions of culture in the context of European manager investing in China through FDI. Scholars have collected a wide number of data at international level in order to measure perceptions of diversity, differences, "cultural distance" and "psychic distance" of managers operating abroad (e.g., Hofstede 1980; Kogut and Singh 1988; Child et al. 2009). Cultural distance and psychic distance are sometimes considered by international business scholars as synonyms, while some other time one being the sub-dimension of the other (e.g., Kogut and Singh 1988; Child et al. 2009). They refer to the distance which is perceived between the home country and the host country's characteristics. With respect to their definition, they differ in terms of levels: While some scholars refer to them at country level, especially "cultural distance" (Hofstede 1980), some others narrow down the definition at individual level (Shenkar 2001). These scholars successfully contributed to the literature by increasing the resources about distance issues; therefore, they can be considered as pillars in international business, cross-cultural management, and social psychology. However, they did not deal with the upside of cultural differences. This chapter fills the void by shedding light on the opportunities generated from cultural diversity in the context of European FDI to China, whose importance as a fruitful market of opportunities is not only confirmed by the figures reported by worldwide investment reports (e.g., UNCTAD 2017) but also by the number of European funded projects involving its relationships with Europe (e.g., European Union Seventh Framework Programme, Horizon 2020). More specifically, we would like to take the challenge of measuring perceptions of culture and focus on individuals who operate abroad, such as country managers, international entrepreneurs, agents), so our analysis is conducted at individual level.

2 Theoretical Background

This chapter draws attention on managers' perceptions of differences and distance between home country and host country, which means that we refer to the degree of familiarity or unfamiliarity perceived by international managers when doing business abroad. Such terminology as "psychic distance" and "cultural distance" belongs to the international business area, while social psychologists generally use the expressions "cultural differences" and exclude "psychic distance" (Mantovani 1998, 2006; Hannerz 2001; Sciortino 2003; Ambos and Håkanson 2014; Johanson and Vahlne 2009; Shenkar 2001; Zaheer et al. 2012). For the purpose of this chapter, we aim at integrating these two perspectives and provide a more comprehensive overview of the concept of culture, on the one hand by drawing on social and cultural psychology theoretical foundation and on the other hand, by providing the definition of culture according to our interviewed managers.

The managers' perceptions analyzed in this study are contextualized within the cross-cultural business setting of European FDI to China.

The Russian scholars are considered the pioneers of the studies on culture, starting from Vygotskij (1934, 1978), who is one of the main pillars in social psychology. Accordingly, culture is considered a source of generation of thoughts and knowledge. Vygotskij (1978) paves the way to his followers on the topic, which is further developed by more recent scholars, such as Anolli (2004), Mantovani (1998, 2006, 2007) and Van Dijk (2008).

Building on the literature on cultural psychology, we draw upon Mantonavi's (2006) and Vygotskij's (1934, 1978) dynamic definition of culture, which refers to the systems of mediation enabling individuals to interact between them and within a specific physical environment. A specific time in the past which identifies when culture was created is not retrievable since culture has always been with us, it is our way of living. Following this perspective, in communication the practice of mediation is intrinsically included within the term "culture." According to Anolli (2004), culture means "sharing" and participation, we are all plunged in a specific culture and in turn, we contribute to build it (Cole 1996; Mantovani 2007). Every culture finds its expression through beliefs, individuals' conducts, everyday practices, forms of expressions such as language or art. These instruments are called artifacts (Vygotskij 1978; Cole 1996) and are used to implement individual activities. These elements refer to tangible objects such as computers, books (material artifacts) as well as institutions, such as education and family (immaterial artifacts). Material and immaterial artifacts enable individuals to get through reality (Mantovani 2006).

Kluckhohn and Kroeber (1952) paved the way to this cultural view. After examining at least 150 definitions of culture, the authors developed a wider definition containing a variety of nuances characterizing cultural processes and the creative and selective skills of individuals. According to them, culture is a series of implicit and explicit models of behavior and for the behavior, which are received and conveyed through symbols. Similarily to Mantovani's (2006) view of culture, these symbols include artifacts, which are the materialization of symbols.

Two different views of culture, which go hand in hand, can be identified: the "reification" and the "narrative" view (Mantovani 2006). Reification is the most rooted interpretation of culture and leads to perceptions of distance since differences have to be homologated. This is an ethnocentric, closed and static view of culture. This is the case of home country firms exporting their business model and imposing it to their branches in the host country. The reification view of culture presupposes homologation as the right approach.

The narrative view to accept and adopt compared to the reification view of culture. This interpretation highlights positivity and fosters a symmetric encounter between two different cultures. Furthermore, it leads to appreciate the benefits of diversity and differences and aims at generating value from them. This is an open view of culture, which is particularly meaningful in cross-cultural business contexts and refers to an open attitude adopted by home country managers toward their host county counterparts.

While Baerveldt and Voestermans (2005) emphasize the concept of "sharing" the same language, knowledge, practices, norms, and values, Van Dijk (2008) proposes to replace the term "culture" with "context." The author argues that it is necessary to narrow down the boundaries of the meaning of culture in order to better grasp the concept. This is the reason why he tends to avoid the wider and indefinite concept of sharing and sheds lights to very specific features and levels, such as context and language. Along with Van Dijk (2008), Lewin (1951) supports the importance of the context by arguing that behavior is a joint function of individuals and their environment, hence context.

Anthropologists have developed a more dynamic definition of culture over the years, shedding light on specific concepts such as

Table 1 Child et al.'s multidimensional model of psychic distance

Geographical Distance	Culture	Language
Level of education	Technological development	Economic development
Logistical infrastructure	Political system	Legal system
Regulations	Accepted business practices	Business ethics

Adapted from Child et al. (2009)

contamination, recomposition, and differentiation to be applied in a profitable and proactive way. For the purpose of this chapter, we support that definition of culture which mirrors these most recent and positive interpretations by adopting the narrative view of culture (Mantovani 2006).

3 Methodology

The data collection regarding managers' perceptions of culture in the context of European FDI to China occurred in the fieldwork—in China—and in a two-step process. Top managers of 18 companies operating in the environmental industry constituted our target. They were submitted a questionnaire covering several sections, from which we extrapolated the key questions: first, the operationalization model of the multidimensional concept of psychic distance (Child et al. 2009); second, the open-ended question about the meaning of culture.

As about the two steps, we combined a quantitative and qualitative data collection process. First, we relied on our 18 managers and detected their perceptions along the psychic distance dimensions. They graded their perceptions on a Likert scale based on five points. Second, we conducted an in-depth analysis on the concept of culture by gathering responses by 7 out of 18 managers.

In order to measure managers' perceptions, we built on the international business literature and used Child et al. (2009) operationalization model of psychic distance, which is a multidimensional construct composed of 12 dimensions (Table 1):

Psychic distance is defined by the authors as the distance perceived by managers between the characteristics of the firms' home country and those of the firms' host country. Two aspects are considered. On the one hand, the *differences* that managers perceive along each dimension and on the other hand, how much each dimension is perceived to *impact* the business activity with the host country. In our case, we concentrate the perceived differences. Our managers graded their perceptions on a 5-point Likert scale. Our target was composed by 18 European managers operating in China whom we met personally during our fieldwork in Beijing and Shanghai in 2014.

Italy, The Netherlands, Belgium, Germany, Spain, and France were the managers' home countries. We reached our respondents thanks to the international fairs held in Beijing during our visiting period and through European embassies and local associations. Due to the reason mentioned in the introduction by Cattaneo (2014) regarding the challenges in collecting data, the small target of respondents is due to the difficulties experienced in China in terms of data availability and a general skeptical attitude toward surveys conducted by universities and research institutes. Our contacts within the companies were initially approached by e-mail, which we sent before traveling. In this way, we explored their willingness to participate in our survey aimed at analyzing Sino-European FDI flows in the environmental industry from three perspectives, legal, economic, and technical engineering. Our team was part of the economic research area. The institutions and embassies based in Beijing enabled us to have a trustful reference when interacting with the companies on-site. Once becoming familiar with the local context and networks, we acquainted and spoke with those European managers willing to participate in our academic survey.

Based on the psychic distance model, we asked them how much difference they perceived between their home country and China along each dimension. Results showed that culture was the most relevant one followed by language. Our managers perceived the biggest difference between home and host country along these two dimensions, which are strongly connected. The third most important dimension was geographical distance.

Second, we conducted an in-depth analysis among seven out of 18 managers. They were asked what "culture" means to them in the form of an open-ended question, which was examined by adopting a social psychology perspective. The following section illustrates the most relevant answers regarding the meaning of culture.

4 Data Analysis

The definitions given by our managers included the following expressions related to culture: a "*common way of thinking of a group of people,*" "*how people see and interpret the world,*" "*how they behave to pursue their own values,*" "*individual/collective values and practices,*" "*communication and codes.*" Such features as "*personal beliefs,*" "*habits,*" "*cultural practice,*" "*religion,*" and "*knowledge acquisition before traveling*" appeared also in the replies. European managers shared some cultural knowledge with other distant countries and with the host culture before approaching China; therefore, they were able to express a series of opinions and comparisons. They showed attention and awareness toward certain cultural traits which do not belong to their home country. They were aware about China's "*achievements through time and history*" as well as other society aspects, which do not belong to their home country. They expressed their most relevant aspects about culture, regarding China and also other "distant" countries: "*society aspects (e.g., casts in India), economical aspects, age, hierarchical position and family (e.g., in Egypt).*" These expressions show managers' awareness about other cultures' priorities with respect to certain values, such as the debate regarding the dualism between career and family.

Two of our respondents share the same view in terms of "*time and history*" when defining culture, for example the "*big achievements of a country,*" "*the natural or man-maid disasters,*" as well as "*religion and doctrines.*" Culture has a specific position in time and space and depends on the nature of individual behavior and how individuals relate with one another.

The importance of the education system and the presence of international schools for children in the host country where they do business emerged in the definitions as a relevant aspect. They got accustomed to the idea that there are many valuable cultures in the world—other than their own—and children "*live better thanks to this.*" Having their children exposed to intercultural stimuli during their childhood is considered fundamental in order to develop openness toward other cultures. The business aspect is combined with the managers' family values.

We were provided with definitions containing Chinese culture-bound terms and references to local habits and customs as well as believes. For example, the presence of a little Buddha or the use of numbers meaning "good luck" is a must in the office as well as *feng shui*, which is related to the design of the office or the company premises. Next to this, *Guanxi* (关系) is another Chinese culture-bound emerging from the replies, which is a term describing the basic dynamics in interpersonal networks. European managers expressed their awareness on the fact that "*culture is very important in international business relations*" in China.

Culture was also described as "*a way of viewing things that happen around us and how we react to them,*" "*a common behavior to be held in common situations,*" "*not a compulsory rule but a wide accepted and recognized manners,*" "*a set of habits as something in which we are born.*" The same respondent applied the meaning of culture to a wide range of life context which go beyond business such as "*food, drinks, interpersonal relations, sport, education.*"

The concept was also linked to specific levels: "*national level, specific regions and provinces or larger areas,*" such as "*Europe,*" "*Middle East,*" "*Western and Eastern cultures.*" The definition provided by our respondents can be linked to Child et al. (2009) model since they included "*language,*" "*communication with the counterpart,*" "*business practices,*" and "*business ethics*" in their meaning of culture.

"*Knowledge of and attention to the cultural differences of the approached market*" appeared in the definitions as crucial to manage intercultural issues on-site: knowledge of the host country values, behavior models, business practices as well as management practices and styles. Also, adapting the business model to the host country and avoiding the ethnocentric perspective are key in dealing with cross-cultural issues in the host country.

One of our respondents provided a lexicographic definition of culture as an intellectual and cognitive knowledge. This knowledge is acquired through prior studies and experience, personally re-elaborated at cognitive level and applied to the in-context situation. On the one hand, this definition was linked to the business activity: Culture concerns the study of products, quality of production, and internationalization. Educating intermediates and agents who work in the host country on behalf of the entrepreneur is part of the knowledge process when doing business abroad. On the other hand, the definition covers the concept of strategic culture, according to which, it is necessary to share the home country business model with the counterparts and discuss it together in order to make adjustments with the host country local culture. Sharing rather than keeping it for the investing counterpart is a crucial step toward integration and success in cross-cultural business contexts. The purpose of this perspective is to enrich the host culture with a combined adjusted business model.

The definitions of culture provided by our respondents showed the high level of managers' awareness on key issues, such as the importance of combining and converging business and family values in the activity abroad, the openness toward the host country local culture and the concept of sharing within in-context situations. All these elements brought our managers to be successful in the host country with their achievements in their business activities and relations. With respect to intercultural communication, one of our respondents showed his cultural awareness and openness derived from prior experiences: *"Being French, which is, unfortunately truly, often a meaning of arrogance and only self interest, I need to be even more careful."* Free cognitive schemas lie behind this expression, which in turn presupposes an observation of reality from a relative rather than absolute perspective.

5 Discussion

Over the past couple of decades, scholars have elaborated a number of concepts linked to "culture" such as "cultural competence" and "cultural sensitivity" (Johnson et al. 2006; Earley 2002; Khanna 2014; Thompson 2002). They are considered key ingredients in cross-cultural settings since these competences help managers to fill the gap between home and host culture. Findings show that managers have acquired those competences and tools by prior experience in the field and personal knowledge, which then lead them to successful practices in Sino-European business contexts. Behind the above-mentioned expressions, we can find some common constructs related to cognition, affection, motivation, and behavior. Combined together, they shape those necessary cross-cultural skills and knowledge which home country managers need to perform effectively and successfully in the host country.

5.1 Cultural Competences and Skills

Johnson et al. (2006) concept of "cultural competence" is determined by a set of skills, knowledge, and attributes. Cultural competence is influenced by "ethnocentrism" and "cultural distance" in business contexts. Ethnocentrism has a negative effect on an individual's ability to respond appropriately to cultural differences in the workplace. For example, Hofstede (2001) refers to "institutional ethnocentrism" having implications at individual level as well as at organizational level. In the context of international business, companies' ethnocentrism is defined as the headquarter imposing on affiliates abroad its "way of working" and business practices. It represents the persistence of structures, processes and management mentalities imposed by the parent organization, even when it is not an appropriate and successful approach. Considering this way of doing business, cultural competence can be defined as a measure used to assess the appropriate and effective use of cross-cultural knowledge, skills, and attitudes in an international business context. With respect to our findings, the lexicographic definition of culture provided by one of our managers supports this argumentation, pinpointing the value of sharing the headquarter business model and discusses it with the host country counterpart before implementing the business activity in the host culture.

Hofstede (2001) and LaFromboise et al. (1993) highlight the intercultural communication competence. According to Hofstede (2001), this competence involves a mixture of awareness, knowledge, and skills. Personality factors also affect the intercultural competence, and LaFromboise et al. (1993) propose a series of key competences, such as negotiating the institutional structures of a specific culture, maintaining active social relations within the cultural group, clear communication, displaying sensitivity, knowledge of beliefs and values. The fact that personality factors affect intercultural communication can be found in one of our respondents' reply: *"Being French, which is, unfortunately truly, often a meaning of arrogance and only self interest, I need to be even more careful."* This cultural awareness and openness derived from prior experiences, which may have shaped the personality of the manager in dealing with cross-cultural contexts.

Achieving such a cultural sensitivity enables to negotiate a common understanding which is of strategic importance in international business settings (Shapiro et al. 2008). Finally, "cultural confidence" can be defined as the ability to understand and master cross-cultural business situations, persevere and being able to do the right things when needed (Earley and Mosakowski 2004). In other words, cultural confidence represents the set of skills, which our target managers need to learn in our proposed intercultural laboratory.

5.2 The *Sociocognitive* Value of the Intercultural Laboratory

Based on the support of our data and on the contributions of social psychology, we propose an intercultural laboratory addressed to early-step international managers. The aim is to provide sociocognitive tools to rethink diversity and capitalizing on cultural differences existing between home country and host country.

The proposed intercultural laboratory would be developed in a series of classes based on group works. Studies supporting the efficacy of cultural trainings date back to more than 10 years ago. Leiba-O'Sullivan's study (1999) shows that such a training improved expatriates' performances since it enables participant to learn the necessary skills that will make cross-cultural relationships easier by reducing misunderstandings and inappropriate behaviors. We can also find detailed contributions in social psychology. In such individualistic cultures like the European, developing cognitive, relational and personal competences in social interactions are fundamental skills to support the *do it with the others' way*-approach rather than *do it on your own-way* (Triandis 1995). Lewin (1951), Bion (1961), and Lai (1973) are some of the pillars on group dynamics as a teaching instrument to learn and educate participants for the sake of the social construction of knowledge. These social psychologists support the social interaction and the communicative exchange in the learning process (Quaglino et al. 1992). Basically, intercultural laboratory is based on intergroup dynamics and relations (Sumner 1906; Turner 1975; Brewer 2003).

Vygotskji (1934) paved the way in highlighting the importance of the sociocognitive value in learning processes to his followers, such as Mugny and Carugati (1987). More specifically, Pontecorvo et al. (1991) followed up these studies on *sociocognitive* conflict and on construction of knowledge (Galli 1976; Pojaghi 2000a, b, 2002, 2008). The reasons of the efficacy of working in groups are the exchange occurring within the interpersonal relations. The positive role of such group dynamics play a crucial and positive role in the proposed intercultural laboratory. By splitting up the class in several groups, members benefit from each others' skills, get acquainted with people's different values, discuss with each other on specific assignments and construct their knowledge through conflicts (Nicolini and Pojaghi 2000). With respect to this training context, "conflict" deserves particular attention. Generally speaking, conflict is considered something to avoid but at the same time we are also skeptical about reaching consensus and cohesion in negotiations and deals. Scholars argue that the term conflict has a double interpretation and usage. On the one hand, it can be considered as negative and a synonym of crisis, break-up. On the other hand, it can be positive because it intrinsically refers to opportunities for dialogue, room for change, creativity and new ideas (Pojaghi 2000a, b).

The effectiveness of the group works lies in the inter-individual assigned activities, which enable to raise managers' awareness on the priority to adopt a relative rather than an absolute view of the world, cooperative attitudes rather than conformism attitudes. Direct confrontation between groups constitutes an opportunity and at the same time an exercise for the members of the different groups. The core of the training resides in the positive meaning of "conflict," room for change, capitalizing on differences between groups rather than homologating those differences. Next to this, listening to the others' viewpoints and explaining one's own point of view by using appropriate languagev are core strengths of the group work. Group members should be trained in "losing" something in order to leave some room and being able to "gain" something in exchange. In order to take advantage from groups' *conflicts,* it is necessary to explain, restructure one's own thoughts and make one's point of view understandable to the others. Every single member of the group should coordinate together and contribute to reach the same objective, which is the common objective of the group. This is what we call awareness of *interdependence*. In this way, the individual gets accustomed to the peer-to-peer cooperation and fosters the construction of knowledge (Moscovici and Doise 1991; Quaglino et al. 1992). Developing such an awareness fosters the elaboration of social stimuli, understanding how the world can be represented and interpreted. Similarly, it is an effective strategy to prevent certain counterproductive social dynamics such as prejudice, stereotyping, and categorization (Nicolini and Pojaghi 2000; Pojaghi 2000a, b).

5.3 Cultural Laboratory Syllabus

The proposed intercultural laboratory should be developed in two steps and coordinated by a person with group leadership and coordination skills, good command of intercultural issues and free cognitive schemas as well as good knowledge of the home country and host country cultural characteristics. In the first step, the aim is to let the participants work together to break the cognitive and sociocultural schemas in the relationships with one other through inter-individual activities. In the second step, the purpose is the co-construction of elements representing the cultural differences emerging between home country and host country. Multimedia material disclosed by the coordinator and free association enable participants to work at cognitive level on the co-existence of numerous ways to interpret reality and business dynamics.

On the basis of a cooperative logic rather than competitiveness between groups, participants' activities are focused on adopting strategies and look for opportunities and integration between groups. Rather than focusing on activities aimed at making decisions for the benefit of one's own group, members of the different groups should leverage on opportunities and integration strategies for the benefit of all the counterparts. More specifically, the first part is aimed at the identification of common sense of theories on (1)"one's own culture," (2) the "other's culture," and (3) differences between the two cultures. This theoretical work is followed by (a) confronting and discussing the different perspectives adopted by participants and (b) attributing meaning to the emerged cultural differences. After detecting cultural differences, challenges and barriers, in the second part of the laboratory, participants work on the co-construction of elements by adopting a cooperative and non-competitive approach, which is aimed at integrating cultural differences and capture opportunities. To conclude, group simulations are foreseen to identify solutions to the challenges and cultural clashes which emerged in the previous activities among partners and members having a different cultural background.

6 Conclusion

This chapter highlights how challenging is the "dialogue" in cross-cultural business settings. Our data collected in the described Sino-European business context show how relevant is the cultural dimension to those European managers working in China. The intercultural laboratory, which we proposed and illustrated in this work, could be a pragmatic tool and a practical suggestion for companies investing abroad. This kind of training aimed at raising managers' awareness at a socio-cognitive level, could become a "structured business practice" adopted by multinational firms, in which everyday working activities are based on choices and decisions made by managers having different cultural backgrounds.

Cultural differences are like a two-sided coin. On the one hand, diversities may lead individuals to take "distance" from them and on the other hand, diversity can be seen as an "opportunity" to enrich both home country and host country counterparts. It is necessary to think outside the box in order to appreciate diversity emerging from cultural encounters. Such an intercultural laboratory would help raise managers' awareness on integration—rather than homologation—of diversities and by leveraging on cooperation—rather than competitiveness among partners—belonging to different cultures. The core of this training is to educate home country managers to rethink and restructure their cognitive rigid schemas by interacting and discussing with the new business setting in the host country.

The inability of international managers to tackle positively the cultural challenges seems to be one of the primary causes of failure. This is most likely due to the low awareness of managers to leverage the cultural challenges that they face in doing business abroad. This "dialogue" challenge can be found not only among managers but also among scholars. In the case of managers, it is about the dialogue between practitioners having different cultural backgrounds (e.g., European and Chinese managers). In the case of scholars, such a challenging dialogue occurs between two different research areas (e.g., international business and social psychology). It is about terminology (e.g., cultural "differences" is used in social psychology, while cultural "distance" in international business).

References

Adler, N. J., & Bartholomew, S. (1992). Academic and professional communities of discourse: Generating knowledge on transnational human resource management. *Journal of International Business Studies, 23*(3), 551–569.

Adler, N. J., Graham, J. L., & Schwarz Gherke, T. (1987). Business negotiations in Canada, Mexico, and the United States. *Journal of Business Research, 15*(5), 411–429.

Allport, G. W. (1954). *The nature of prejudice*. Cambridge, MA: Addison-Wesley.

Ambos, B., & Håkanson, L. (2014). The concept of distance in international management research. *Journal of International Management, 20*(1), 1–7.

Anolli, L. (2004). *Psicologia della cultura*. Bologna: Il Mulino.

Arfelli Galli, A. (1997). *Didattica interattiva e formazione degli insegnanti*. Bologna: Clueb.

Baerveldt, C., & Voestermans, P. (2005). Culture, emotions, and the normative structure of reality. *Theory and Psychology, 15*(4), 449–473.
Bass, B. M. (1990). *Handbook of leadership: A survey of theory and research*. New York: Free Press.
Besemeres, M., & Wierzbicka, A. (Eds.). (2008). *Translating lives: Living with two languages and cultures*. Queensland: University of Queensland Press.
Billing, M. (1996). *Discutere e pensare. Un approccio retorico alla psicologia sociale*. Milano: Cortina.
Bion, W. R. (1961). *Esperienze nei gruppi*. Roma: Armando.
Brewer, M. B. (1979). In-group bias in the minimal intergroup situation: A cognitive-motivational analysis. *Psychological Bulletin, 86*(2), 307–324.
Brewer, M. B. (1981). Ethnocentrism and its role in intergroup trust. In M. Brewer & B. Collins (Eds.), *Scientific inquiry in the social sciences* (pp. 214–231). San Francisco: Jossey-Bass.
Brewer, M. B. (1999). The psychology of prejudice: Ingroup love or outgroup hate? *Journal of Social Issues, 55*(3), 429–444.
Brewer, M. B. (2003). *Intergroup relations*. Berkshire: Free University Press.
Brouthers, K. D., & Brouthers, L. E. (2000). Acquisition or greenfield startup? Institutional, cultural and transaction cost influences. *Strategic Management Journal, 21*(1), 89–97.
Callari Galli, M. (2004). Cultura e contemporaneità. Nuovi scenari per un concetto compromesso. *Rassegna Italiana di Sociologia, 1*, 21–37.
Cattaneo, M. (2014). Elogio alla diversità. *Le Scienze, 556*, 9–9.
Child, J., Rodrigues, S. B., & Frynas, J. G. (2009). Psychic distance, its impact and coping modes: Interpretations of SMEs decision-makers. *Management International Review, 49*(2), 199–224.
Coin, R. (2001). *Psicologia sociale e interculturale*. Milano: Cortina.
Cole, M. (1996). *Cutural psychology. A once and future discipline*. Cambridge, MA: The Belknap Press of Harvard University Press.
Cucino, D., Rodemer, T., & Bouée, C. E. (2013). *European chamber of commerce in China, Chinese outbound investment in the European union*. Beijing: European Chamber.
Earley, P. C. (2002). Redefining interactions across cultures and organizations: Moving forward with cultural intelligence. *Research in Organizational Behavior, 24*, 271–299.
Earley, P. C., & Ang, S. (2003). *Cultural intelligence: Individual interactions across cultures*. Stanford, CA: Stanford Business Books.

Earley, C. P., & Mosakowski, E. (2004). Cultural intelligence. *Harvard Business Review, 82*(10), 139–146.

Evans, J., Treadgold, A., & Mavondo, F. T. (2000). Explaining export development through psychic distance. *International Marketing Review, 17*(2), 164–168.

Fabietti, U. (1995). *L'identità etnica*. Roma: Carocci.

Fairclough, N. L. (1995). *Critical discourse analysis: The critical study of language*. Longman: Harlow.

Farr, R. M., & Moscovici, S. (1984). *Social representations*. Cambridge: Cambridge University Press.

Fayollea, A., Basso, O., & Boucharda, V. (2010). Three levels of culture and firms' entrepreneurial orientation: A research agenda. *Entrepreneurship and Regional Development, 22*(7–8), 707–730.

Grieve, P. G., & Hogg, M. A. (1999). Subjective uncertainty and intergroup discrimination in the minimal group situation. *Personality and Social Psychology Bulletin, 25*(8), 926–940.

Galli G. (1976). *Didattica universitaria e professione: esperienze in una Facoltà umanistica (1964–1966, 1974–1975)*. Padova: Antenore.

Geertz, C. (1973). *The interpretation of cultures*. New York: London Basic Books.

Gertsen, M. C. (1990). Intercultural competence and expatriates. *International Journal of Human Resources Management, 11*(3), 341–362.

Gillespie, A. (2008). Social representations, alternative representations and semantic barriers. *Journal for the Theory of Social Behaviour, 38*(4), 376–391.

Guretl, F. (2014). L'equazione dell'inclusione. Scienza e tecnologia sono le principali forze motrici della prosperità sociale. Ma chi riesce ad arrivare al posto di guida? *Le Scienze [Italian version of Scientific American], 556*, 36–39.

Hannerz, U. (1992). *Cultural complexity*. New York: Columbia University Press.

Hannerz, U. (2001). *La diversità culturale*. Bologna: Il Mulino.

Hanemann, T. (2014, December). *The new complexity of Chinese outbound investment*. Rhodium Group. http://rhg.com/notes/the-new-complexity-of-chinese-outbound-investment. Accessed Apr 2017.

Hofstede, G. (1980). *Culture's consequences: International differences in work-related values*. Beverly Hills, CA: Sage.

Hofstede, G. (1994). The business of international business is culture. *International Business Review, 3*(1), 1–14.

Hofstede, G. (2001), *Culture's Consequences: Comparing Values, Behaviors, Institutions, and Organizations Across Nations*. 2nd ed. Thousand Oaks, CA: Sage.
Johanson, J., & Wiedersheim-Paul, F. (1975). The internationalization of the firm—four Swedish cases. *Journal of management studies, 12*(3), 305–323.
Johanson, J., & Vahlne, E. (1977). The internationalization process of the firm: A model of knowledge development and increasing foreign market commitments. *Journal of International Business Studies, 8,* 23–32.
Johanson, J., & Vahlne, J. E. (2009). The uppsala internationalization process model revisited—From liability of foreignness to liability of outsidership. *Journal of International Business Studies, 40,* 1–21.
Johnson, J. P., Lenartowicz, T., & Apud, S. (2006). Cross-cultural competence in international business: Toward a definition and a model. *Journal of International Business Studies, 37*(4), 525–543.
Khanna, T. (2014). Contextual intelligence. *Harvard Business Review, 92*(9), 58–68.
Kluckhohn, C., & Kroeber, A. (1963). *Culture: A critical review of concepts and definitions*. New York: Vintage Books.
Kogut, B., & Singh, H. (1988). The effect of national culture on the choice of entry mode. *Journal of International Business Studies, 19,* 411–432.
Lai, G. (1973). *Gruppi di apprendimento*. Torino: Boringhieri.
LaFromboise, T., Coleman, H. L. K., & Gerton, J. (1993). Psychological impact of biculturalism: Evidence and theory. *Psychological Bulletin, 114*(3), 395–412.
Lanternari, V. (1983). *L' "incivilimento dei barbari": Problemi di etnocentrismo e d'identità*. Bari: Dedalo.
Leiba-O'Sullivan, S. (1999). The distinction between stable and dynamic cross-cultural competencies: Implications for expatriate training. *Journal of International Business Studies, 30*(4), 709–725.
Lewin (1951). In D. Cartwright (ed.), Field theory in social science: Selected theoretical papers by Kurt Lewin. New York: Harper & Row.
Loyd, D. L., Wang, C. S., Phillips, K. W., & Lount, R. B. (2013). Social category diversity promotes premeeting elaboration: The role of relationship focus. *Organization Science, 24*(3), 757–772.
Mantovani, G. (1998). *L'elefante invisibile: Tra negoziazione e affermazione delle diversità. Scontri e incontri multiculturali*. Firenze: Giunti.
Mantovani, G. (2006). Il difficile riconoscimento delle differenze. La necessità di una scelta tra due concezioni incompatibili della cultura. *Psicologia Sociale, 2,* 223–232.

Mantovani, G. (2007). Dalla psicologia culturale alla prospettiva interculturale. In B. Mazzara (Ed.), *Prospettive di psicologia culturale* (pp. 57–76). Roma: Carocci.

Moscovici, S. (1976). *Social influence and social change*. London: Academic Press.

Moscovici, S. (1988). Notes towards a description of social representations. *Journal of European Social Psychology, 18*(3), 211–250.

Moscovici S., & Doise W. (1991). *Dissensi e consensi*. Bologna: Il Mulino.

Mugny, G., & Carugati, F. (Eds.). (1987). *Psicologia sociale dello sviluppo cognitivo*. Firenze: Giunti-Barbera.

Nicolini P., & Pojaghi B. (2000). *Sentimenti, pensieri e pregiudizi nella relazione interpersonale: Il bambino e la conoscenza dell'Altro*. Milan: Franco Angeli.

Novara, D. (1996). L'arte del conflitto per una pedagogia della pace. In *conference proceedings, Scuola di pace "Vincenzo Buccelletti", Senigallia* , Italy, March 1996, 17.

Ozawa, T. (1979). International investment and industrial structure: New theoretical implications from the Japanese experience. *Oxford Economic Papers, 31*(1), 72–92.

Phillips, K. W. (2014). Come funziona la diversità. *Le Scienze [Italian version of Scientific American], 556*, 41–45.

Plaut, V. (2014). Aprire le porte a tutti. *Le Scienze [Italian version of Scientific American], 556*, 50–55.

Pojaghi, B. (2000a). Metacognizione e costruzione sociale della conoscenza. In R. Vianello & M. Tortello (Eds.), *Esperienze di apprendimento cooperativo* (pp. 123–133). Bergamo: Junior.

Pojaghi, B. (2000b). *Il gruppo come strumento di formazione complessa. Il farsi e il disfarsi delle idee*. Milano: Franco Angeli.

Pojaghi, B. (2002). Sperimentare la costruzione sociale della conoscenza nei piccoli gruppi. In Atti III *Biennale internazionale della didattica universitaria* (pp. 135–148). Lecce: Pensa Multimedia.

Pojaghi, B. (2008). Il gruppo di formazione. In S. Porcu (Ed.), *Salute e malattia. Mutamento socio-culturale e trasformazioni organizzative dei servizi alla persona* (pp. 153–169). Milano: Franco Angeli.

Pojaghi, B., & Fermani, A. (2006). La costruzione sociale della conoscenza nella didattica universitaria. In B. Pojaghi & P. Nicolini, (Eds.), *Il rispetto dell'altro nella formazione e nell'insegnamento. Scritti in onore di Anna Arfelli Galli* (pp. 43–62). Macerata: Eum.

Pontecorvo, C., Ajello, A. M., & Zucchermaglio, C. (1991). *Discutendo si impara*. Roma: NIS.
Quaglino, G. P., Casagrande, S., & Castellano, A. (1992). *Gruppo di lavoro, lavoro di gruppo*. Milano: Raffaello Cortina.
Quer, D., Claver, E., & Rienda, L. (2012). Political risk, cultural distance, and outward foreign direct investment: Empirical evidence from large Chinese firms. *Asia Pacific journal of management, 29*(4), 1089–1104.
Rottig, D., & Reus, T. H. (2009). Institutional distance, organizational legitimacy, and the performance of foreign acquisitions in the United States. In *Academy of Management Annual Meeting Proceedings*, (pp. 1–6).
Sciortino, G. (2003). From homogeneity to difference? Comparing multiculturalism as a description and as a field from claim-making. *Comparative Social Research, 22,* 263–285.
Shapiro, J. M., Ozanne, J. L., & Saatcioglu, B. (2008). An interpretive examination of the development of cultural sensitivity in international business. *Journal of International Business Studies, 39*(1), 71–87.
Shenkar, O. (2001). Cultural distance revisited: Towards a more rigorous conceptualization and measurement of cultural differences. *Journal of International Business Studies, 32,* 519–536.
Sherif, M. (1966). *In common predicament, Social psychology of intergroup conflict and cooperation*. New York: Houghton Mifflin.
Sherif, M., & Sherif, C. W. (1953). *Groups in harmony and tension: An integration of studies on intergroup relations*. New York: Harper.
Sousa, C. M., & Bradley, F. (2006). Cultural distance and psychic distance: Two peas in a pod? *Journal of International Marketing, 14*(1), 49–70.
Spigarelli, F. (2010). Chinese investments in Italy: Is the wave arriving? *International Journal of Asian Business and Information Management, 1*(1), 54–76.
Stevens, F. G., Plaut, V. C., & Sanchez-Burks, J. (2008). Unlocking the benefits of diversity: All-inclusive multiculturalism and positive organizational change. *Journal of Applied Behavioural Science. 4,* 116–133.
Stolcke, V. (2000). Le nuove frontiere e le nuove retoriche culturali della esclusione in Europa. In S. Mezzadra, A. Petrillo (Eds.), *I confini della globalizzazione: lavoro, culture, cittadinanza*. Roma: Manifestolibri.
Stöttinger, B., & Schlegelmilch, B. B. (2000). Psychic distance: A concept past its due date? *International Marketing Review, 17*(2), 169–173.
Sumner, W. G. (1906). *Folksways*. New York: Ginn.

Tajfel, H. (1969). Cognitive aspects of prejudice. *Journal of Social Issues, 25,* 79–97.

Tajfel, H. (1981). *Human groups and social categories.* Cambridge: Cambridge University Press.

Tajfel, H., & Wilkes, A. L. (1963). Classification and quantitative judgment. *British Journal of Psychology, 54,* 101–114.

Tajfel, H., Billig, M. G., & Bundy, R. P. (1971). Social categorization and intergroup behaviour. *European Journal of Social Psychology, 1*(2), 149–178.

Teerikangas, S., & Very, P. (2012). Culture in mergers and acquisitions: A critical synthesis and steps forward. In D. Faulkner, S. Teerikangas, & R. J. Joseph (Eds.), *The handbook of mergers and acquisitions.* Oxford: Oxford University Press.

Thompson, C. J. (2002). A re-inquiry on re-inquiries: A postmodern proposal for a critical-reflexive approach. *Journal of Consumer Research, 29*(2), 142–145.

Triandis, H. C. (1995). *Individualism and collectivism.* Boulder, CO: Westview Press.

Turner, J. C. (1975). Social comparison and social identity: Some prospects for intergroup behaviour. *European Journal of Social Psychology, 5,* 5–34.

UNCTAD. (2017, January 28). *Global investment trends monitor* (No. 15). New York: United Nations.

Van Dijk, T. A. (1993). Principles of critical discourse analysis. *Discourse and Society, 4*(2), 249–283.

Van Dijk, T. A. (2008). *Context. Towards a multidisciplinary theory.* Cambridge: Cambridge University Press.

Von Glinow, M. A., Shapiro, D. L., & Brett, J. M. (2004). Can we talk, and should we? Managing emotional conflict in multicultural teams. *Academy of Management Review, 29*(4), 578–592.

Vygotskij, L. S. (1978). *Mind in society: The development of higher psychological processes.* Cambridge, MA: Harvard University Press.

Vygostkij, L. S. (1934). *Pensiero e linguaggio.* Bari: Laterza.

Williams, D. W., & Grégoire, D. A. (2015). Seeking commonalities or avoiding differences? Re-conceptualizing distance and its effects on internationalization decisions. *Journal of International Business Studies, 46*(3), 253–284.

Yoshino, M. Y. (1976). *Japan's multinational enterprises.* Cambridge, MA: Harvard University Press.

Zaheer, S., Schomaker, M. S., & Nachum, L. (2012). Distance without direction: Restoring credibility to a much-loved construct. *Journal of International Business Studies, 43,* 18–27.

4

European Entry Decisions in China: The Role of Cultural Perceptions

Abstract This chapter investigates to what extent and how perceptions of culture affect European investment decisions to China. First, it analyzes managers' perceptions of "culture." Secondly, it examines whether European managers' perceptions are based on a European culture or on national cultures, and whether intra-China cultural differences are considered. We adopt a multiple case study research design composed of a panel of six European companies investing in China in the green tech industry. We use quantitative and qualitative analyses and a three-step data collection process. Results show that: (1) managers' perceptions vary over time, between the pre- and post-market entry operation; (2) the cultural aspect is not considered by European managers before approaching China; (3) only after entering the Chinese market, European managers realize the relevance of culture; (4) they perceive China as a single entity rather than intra-China cultural differences; (5) when approaching China, European managers' perceptions are based on a *national culture* (intra-Europe) rather than a *common European culture;* (6) the cultural dimension goes along with language, which, in specific cases, is perceived as a higher hurdle than culture.

K. Vaccarini et al., *Cultural Distance in International Ventures*,
DOI 10.1007/978-3-319-62193-7_4

Keywords Cultural distance · Psychic distance · Cross cultural Culture · Managers' perceptions · European culture · National culture Intra-China cultural differences · European investment decisions to China · Green tech industry

1 Introduction

Culture is a widely adopted and variedly defined concept in international business, and a consensus about the definition is still quite unclear despite its long tradition (Kluckhohn and Kroeber 1963; Geerzt 1973; Hofstede 1980, 1993, 1994). In this chapter, we recall and adopt Child et al.'s (2009) definition of culture, which we derive from the construct of psychic distance and the way it is operationalized. In doing so, we focus on a more pragmatic and operational construct rather than a theoretical one. With respect to this, it is necessary to point out four key aspects of Child et al.'s (2009) definition of culture: (1) It is a component (distinct from "language") of the more general and multidimensional construct of "psychic distance"; (2) it appears as one of the 12 psychic distance construct dimensions; (3) the authors explicitly keep the dimensions "culture" and "language" separated in the operationalization of the construct; (4) it refers to the concept of "distance." It is well established in international business literature that culture (and language) has an effect on investment decisions of firms expanding abroad (Kogut and Singh 1988; Brouthers and Brouthers 2000; Teerikangas and Very 2012). Recent analyses have integrated and synthesized a substantial body of empirical work on the impact of culture on FDI (Stahl and Voigt 2008; Tihanyi et al. 2005).

As regards the more theoretical aspect of culture, a recent study on social psychology applied to international business highlights the need—and challenge—for international business scholars to integrate social psychological theoretical foundations to international business in order to increase managers' awareness on how to get value from cultural differences (Vaccarini and Pojaghi 2015). Under this perspective, Baerveldt and Voestermans (2005) refer to the concept culture as "sharing"—the same language, knowledge, practices, norms, and values. The operational and theoretical framework adopted in this chapter to detect managers' cultural perceptions is the psychic distance operationalization model elaborated by Child et al. (2009), who borrow the term "psychic" from psychology and the term "distance" from international business (Child et al. 2009; Nebus and Chai 2013; Puthussery et al. 2014; Håkanson et al. 2016). This model includes 12 dimensions,[1] among which "culture" and "language" are perceived as the most relevant ones among our target composed of top managers representing our six companies.

Psychic distance is defined by Child et al. (2009) as the existing perceived distance between the characteristics of the firm's home country and the characteristics of the firm's host country. In this chapter, we adopt the psychic distance sub-dimension "culture" as the main operational construct. We mainly refer to "cultural perceptions" and "cultural differences." Accordingly, cultural differences are defined as the existing perceived differences between the firm's home country and the firm's host country characteristics. This conceptualization focuses on "perceived differences" rather than "perceived distance" and on the individual level since it is based on individual perceptions. Next to the social psychological conceptualization of culture regarding shared values, norms, and beliefs, culture in international business contexts entails a series of country as well as firm-specific characteristics. These features appear as dimensions not only in the psychic distance operationalization model but also in our main findings and are categorized under the names of "accepted business practices" and "business ethics" (Child et al. 2009).

After examining at least 150 definitions of culture, Kluckhohn and Kroeber (1952) developed a wider definition containing a variety of nuances characterizing cultural processes, especially the creative and selective skill of the human being. According to this view, culture is a series of models—implicit and explicit—of behavior and for the behavior, which is received and conveyed through symbols. By applying the core of these definitions (e.g., practices, behavior, and symbols) to business contexts, it can be argued that culture manifests itself in international business settings in the form of specific and "accepted business practices," which is one of the 12 psychic distance dimensions (Child et al. 2009).

Studies on perceptions are reflected in the operationalization of psychic distance conducted by international business scholars (e.g., Stöttinger and Schlegelmilch 2000). They are based on the principles of cognitive mapping and Gestalt psychology as affirmed by Powell and Ansic (1997). Social psychologists show that individuals tend to prefer familiar rather than unfamiliar situations. In this chapter, we incorporate the literature on distance and perceptions in international business. While Child et al. (2009) apply their model to the internationalization of British companies in Brazil, we conduct our research in the context of European green tech investments to China as part of a EU project on renewable energies and environmental industries.[2] Likewise, the focus is on top managers' perceptions as the main decision-makers.

As about the green tech sector, we build on Lv and Spigarelli's (2015) research pinpointing the need to conduct analyses at an industry level in order to contextualize the results. Europe and China are experiencing a strong cooperation in partnering opportunities, especially after the emphasis on the "go global" policies foreseen in the Twelfth Five Year Plan and the number of green relevant policies to specific sectors (Langer and Watson 2004; Aizawa and Yang 2010; Huang and Chen 2015; Lv and Spigarelli 2015). According to the world, China is now the leader in renewable energy investment and that makes the case of China especially relevant and worthy investigation bank (The World Bank and The Development Research Center of the State Council, the People's Republic of China 2013; Pew 2011).

Our research enables us to draw upon primary data collected in the field through a multiple case study, including an in-depth case-based analysis of six European companies that have entered the Chinese market between 2001 and 2014. The top managers of these companies constitute the target of our interviews and part of our data collection process. These six companies operate in the green tech industry—green buildings, green technology, consultancy, solar energy plants, engineering, plumbing, and heating systems.[3]

This chapter aims to answer the following research questions:

1. Which are European top managers' perceptions of culture when investing in China?
2. Do European managers perceive China as culturally homogeneous? Or do they perceive intra-China differences?

This chapter is structured as follows. The theoretical background section illustrates the relevance of culture in the decision making of European firms investing in China. We then describe the methodology of our research, and in the next section, we analyze and discuss the main findings and implications. We conclude our study with final remarks, limitations, and possible directions for future research.

2 Theoretical Background

Studies about cultural differences are mainly conducted at country level and do not look at what individuals perceive; they mainly look "outside" of the individual. The construct of cultural distance is generally analyzed at three main levels: country, firm, and individual level (Hofstede 1980; Forsgren 2002; Cheng 2006; Jiang 2006; Brewer and Venaik 2011; Ambos and Håkanson 2014). The country level focuses on the values and behavior of the society as a whole, the firm level is based on certain business practices, and the individual level concerns the individuals' perceptions of distance.

Building on Child et al.'s (2009) study on the operationalization of psychic distance, from which we derive our concept of culture, we concentrate on the individual level of perceptions of culture. Cultural distance is generally analyzed at three main levels: country, firm, and individual level (Hofstede 1980, 1993, 1994; Forsgren 2002; Cheng 2006; Jiang 2006; Brewer and Venaik 2011; Ambos and Håkanson 2014; Puthussery et al. 2014; Håkanson et al. 2016). The country level focuses on the values and behavior of society as a whole, the firm level is based on business practices, and the individual level on individuals' perceptions. Studies about cultural perceptions are mainly conducted at country level and do not look at what individuals perceive (e.g., Hofstede 1980). Therefore, this chapter fills the void by focusing on what managers perceive.

According to Shenkar (2001), the cultural distance indexes do not apply to investment decisions as they fail to yield consistent empirical evidence and they include some hidden assumptions which are named "illusions," such as the illusions of homogeneity and symmetry. The illusion of homogeneity takes for granted the fact that there is no difference of values in the same country, that is intra-country level. Illusion of symmetry means that the distance perceived from country A toward country B can be different than the distance perceived from country B toward A.

Kroeber and Kluckhohn (1952) identified 164 different definitions of culture. More have been added since then, as the term became more popular in the management literature (Lees 2003). Most researchers use the definition of culture by Hofstede (1980) in reference to national culture, and his subsequent work, and definition of culture (Hofstede 1983) regarding organizational culture, and more recently scholars have based their definition of culture on the work by the "GLOBE" project team, which suggests that "the most parsimonious operationalizations of societal culture consist of commonly experiences language, ideological belief systems (including religion and political belief systems), ethnic heritage, and history" and that "the most parsimonious operationalizations of organizational culture consist of commonly used nomenclature within an organization, shared organizational values, and organizational history" (House et al. 2004: 1516). This definition does not only distinguish two levels of culture, societal (or national), and organizational (or corporate) culture, which are noticeably distinguished in the FDI literature, too. It also illustrates the wide consensus in the literature that language is part of culture.

Next to these studies, international business literature offers a wide spectrum of works on the cultural dimension. Starting with the work of Yoshino (1976) and Ozawa (1979), taking off with the seminal work by Hofstede (1980) that inspired a large body of conceptual and empirical work on the role of culture, the latter of which was further fueled by the "cultural distance" construct developed by Kogut and Singh (1988) (e.g., Brouthers and Brouthers 2000; Pothukuchi et al. 2002; Tihanyi et al. 2005; Reus and Rottig 2009; Rottig et al. 2013; Teerikangas and Very 2012). Recent analyses have integrated and synthesized a substantial body of empirical work on the impact of culture (Stahl and Voigt 2008; Tihanyi et al. 2005). However, to the best of our knowledge, none of these studies focus on entry decisions in the context of Europe–China relationships and at an industrial level, which is in our case, the green tech sector.

Firms' internationalization to emerging markets, such as China, has been examined under different viewpoints and has taken into account a wide range of business contexts and pair countries (e.g., Deng 1997; Gao 2005; Brewer 2007; Zihui et al. 2008). Country's economic history (Tsang 1994; Salavrakos 2010), historical ties (Makino and Tsang 2011), management experience (Hong and Chen 2001), human resource management (Tsang 1994), and trends and determinants (e.g., Ma et al. 2008) are some of the numerous viewpoints adopted by international business scholars.

In the context of international mergers and acquisitions, for example, scholars have employed such theoretical perspectives as attribution theory (e.g., Vaara 2000), the concept of meaning (Weber 1996), organizational learning theory (e.g., Barkema et al. 1996; Olie 1994; Villinger 1996), the theory of relative standing (e.g., Krug and Nigh 1998), the resource-based view as well as knowledge-based view of the firm (e.g., Morosini et al. 1998; Uhlenbruck 2004), social identity and self-categorization theories (e.g., Turner 1975; Vaara et al. 2003; Brewer 2003), and social movements theory (e.g., Veiga et al. 2000).

In this chapter, we draw upon Child et al.'s (2009) study on psychic distance by looking at how the construct is operationalized, which is particularly relevant to us since "culture" is one of the 12 dimensions contained in the model (Table 1):

As regards the operationalization of psychic distance and culture, some scholars use both concepts interchangeably as a synonym, considering them at the same level. Some others use culture as a proxy of psychic distance (e.g., Sousa and Bradley 2006, 2008; Brewer 2007; Puthussery 2014). More specifically, building on recent studies (Child et al. 2002, 2009) on psychic distance and international business, we refer to culture as a "sub-dimension" of the wider psychic distance

Table 1 Child et al.'s psychic distance dimensions

Geographical distance	Culture	Language
Level of Education	Technological development	Economic development
Logistical Infrastructure	Political System	Legal System
Regulations	Accepted Business Practices	Business Ethics

Adapted from Child et al. (2009)

construct, which is defined by Child et al. (2009: 201) as the existing perceived distance between the characteristics of a firm's home country and a foreign country of entry, or contemplating, doing business or investing. We draw from Child et al.'s (2009) operationalization and conceptualization of psychic distance to refer to the pragmatic meaning of culture, which we adopt for the purpose of this study. Our focus is on cultural perceptions and differences rather than distance. We think that Child et al.'s (2009) model is a comprehensive one since the authors derive its operationalization and conceptualization from previous empirical and theoretical studies (e.g., Gehmawat 2001; Child et al. 2002).

Earlier studies postulated a number of dimensions that might enter into psychic distance, such as differences in culture, language, political and legal systems, level of education, industrial development, and business practices (e.g., Carlson 1974; Johanson and Vahlne 1977; Johanson and Wiedersheim-Paul 1975). On the one hand, the theoretical aspect is referred to the overall framework within which the 12 dimensions are located, which is Gehmawat's (2001) "CAGE" classification of distance. Cultural, administrative, geographic, and economic factors constitute this framework, which is a relatively comprehensive classification. The cultural dimension includes differences in language and social norms; the administrative includes differences in political system, government policies, and institutions; and the economic dimension entails differences in income levels, infrastructure, human, and other resources. On the other hand, the empirical studies from which the 12 dimensions are derived refer to the internationalization of Hong Kong firms (Child et al. 2002). The main findings emerging from this empirical research showed several recurring dimensions which served as a basis for the psychic distance operationalization model (Child et al. 2009).

As regards the individual level of analysis, the focus of this chapter is managers' perceptions of culture. We refer to the individual and the cognitive dimensions, which play a significant role in managers' perceptions and understanding of the host country's foreign environment and its characteristics (Billing 1996; Evans et al. 2000; Cattaneo 2014). The cognitive dimension has been neglected over the years (Evans et al. 2000; Child et al. 2009: 200); we fill this void by conducting an in-depth analysis on cognition and go beyond the "objective" features of the national level of analysis: Attention is drawn to what the individuals perceive.

The cultural dimension in psychic distance applies to a series of cases, such as human resource management and business behavior. To define culture, we draw upon scholars' studies from international business and social psychology. Hofstede (1993, 1994) refers to a series of items, such as values, ideas, symbols, and beliefs which are shared by a group of people. He defines the construct as a collective mental programing. Furthermore, culture can be identified as a combination of acquired experience and values that contribute to and influence distinctive groups' behavior and responses (Johnson and Turner 2004).

By adopting a social psychological perspective and according to cultural theories, culture is a set of mediation systems enabling human beings to interact between them and within a specific physical environment (Mantovani 2006; Vygotskij 1934, 1978). This means participation as well as "sharing" (Cole 1996; Anolli 2004; Mantovani 2007). Every culture finds its expression through beliefs, values, individuals' conducts, everyday practices, and forms of expressions, such as language or art. Baerveldt and Voestermans (2005) associate the concept of culture with "sharing" the same language, knowledge, practices, norms, and values.

Van Dijk (2008) sheds lights on the "context," proposing to avoid the term "culture." The author argues that it is necessary to narrow the boundaries of its meaning of culture in order to grasp the concept. This is the reason why he tends to avoid the wider and indefinite concept of sharing, referring to more pragmatic features and levels, such as context, and language.

Previous studies on psychic distance have focused on differences between countries and mainly relied on questionnaire survey data (e.g., Klein and Roth 1990), experts (e.g., Dow 2000), or national indicators (e.g., Dow and Karunaratna 2006). They lacked in investigating the cognition of decision-makers (Stöttinger and Schlegelmilch 2000). With this chapter, we contribute to draw attention to the "psychic" rather than the "distance" side of the psychic distance construct. Within this framework, culture is analyzed at individual level considering the crucial role of the decision-makers, whose perceptions and skills in facing cultural issues may affect the internationalization process of the firm (Harzing 2003; Brewer 2007; Child et al. 2009; Hashim 2012).

We examine managers' perceptions of culture at individual level in terms of (1) "perceived cultural difference between home and host country" and (2) "perceived impact that the cultural dimension has on the businesses with the host country."

3 Methodology

3.1 Multiple Case Study Research Design

We adopted a multiple case study research design which provides a deep and explorative understanding of managers' perceptions of culture in entry decisions and is particularly suited for inductive theory development (Yin 2014). Case studies provide deep and rich knowledge and information about emerging issues that cannot yet be explained in a deductive way due to lack of a theoretical basis.

Data about European managers' perceptions were collected in the fieldwork in 2014. Firstly, we submitted a questionnaire[4] to a sample of 22 respondents. Secondly, we asked 6 out of these 22 managers to reply to an open-ended question regarding the meaning of culture in order to go deeper into the understanding of the concept. The data collection process relied on the presence of at least two researchers in China, who implemented and carried out the investigation from the pre-travel to the post-travel phase. This process enabled us to keep more rigorous and careful data due to the cooperation in the fieldwork, the multiple sources of evidence (companies' Web sites and publicly available documents), a shared database, maintenance and chain of evidence in the form of notes, documents, e-mail exchanges, tabular, and narrative material.

Compared to a single case study, a multiple case study provides better opportunities for comparisons, as well as a variety of research sites and data sources to formulate propositions, theory generation, and cross-case study analyses (Patton 1990; Eisenhardt 1989; Yin 1994, 2003).

In our chapter, we aim at providing a descriptive analysis and a combination of quantitative and qualitative approaches, from Likert scale-based questions to open-ended questions (Bourgeois and Eisenhardt 1988, 1989). The open-ended question and the qualitative analysis enable us to capture nuances on managers' perceptions (Stöttinger and Schlegelmilch 2000).

3.2 Data Collection Process

Our data collection process developed in three steps in terms of time scheduling: (1) pre-travel, (2) fieldwork, and (3) post-travel. We gathered two types of data in the form of a questionnaire (quantitative), interviews and open-ended questions (qualitative). A detailed description of our protocol follows.

The questionnaire and the interviews covered three main areas, namely economics—with a specific focus on culture—law, and engineering.[5] We obtained 22 responses and extracted the most significant answers in compliance with our cultural perspective of analysis, by means of a Likert scale based on 5 points and "yes/no" questions.

The open-ended questions were the following ones: (a) "what does culture mean for you?", (b) "how would you define your company entry mode in the Chinese market (e.g. FDI, direct or indirect export, licensing, franchising, joint venture, etc.)?", (c) "was the entry mode choice influenced by cultural, financial, technical/practical, bureaucratic, legal or other aspects?". After getting the 22 questionnaires, in order to have a deeper understanding of managers' perceptions of culture, we addressed the above-mentioned open-ended questions to a short-listed sample of six managers.

In the pre-travel phase, we drew up a full contact list of company associations, firms and governmental organizations, and national and international institutions, operating in the green tech industry and involving European and Chinese investments. During this step, the project coordinator and the team members established a first e-mail contact with these entities by sending out a cover letter containing our research purposes and the link to our online questionnaire.

More specifically, before our departure to China (Beijing and Shanghai 2014), we e-mailed European national organizations based both in Europe and in China, European embassies in Beijing, and associations providing support for European small and medium enterprises in China.[6]

In the fieldwork, two members of our team arranged video calls, face to face meetings, and on-site company visits. All these activities, topics of the meetings, and interviews were recorded in the official report addressed to the European Union.[7]

In order to have direct access to the companies without involving third parties, we attended some international fairs to find managers representing their respective companies at the stands. Furthermore, we arranged meetings with academic institutions[8] in order to have scholars' perspectives and to keep us informed about ongoing research projects on the topics. In this regard, economists, engineers, and legal members of our team (about 60 researchers) took part in international business conferences on European and Chinese FDI flows.[9]

The post-travel step consisted in a preliminary analysis of the data collected on-site and of the open-ended questions regarding the meaning of culture and the entry mode choice.

4 Analysis and Discussion

Table 2 shows the company profiles of our multiple case study sample (6 short-listed out of 22) represented by the interviewed managers.

Table 2 Company profiles

	Company A	Company B	Company C	Company D	Company E	Company F
Year of establishment	2001	2014	2013	2009	2006	2009
Respondents' position and nationality	Brand Ambassador, Dutch	CEO, Italy	General Manager, Turkish	Sales and Projects Manager (China), Belgian	Asia Executive Director, Spanish	General Manager, Chinese
FDI entry mode	Joint venture	Merger and acquisition	WOFE	Branch	Joint venture	WOFE
Turnover in China (USD)	48,000,000	113,000	3,800,000	90,000,000	74,000,000	N/A[a]
Core business	Manuf. revolving doors	Service: consultancy, service, information and communication	Manuf. heating business	Manuf. and services: turnkeyprojects, engineering	Manuf. and service: energy plant developer, engineering, and operation	R&D: applied research, product development, engineering support
Headquarter location	Netherlands	Italy	United Kingdom	Belgium	Spain	France
Chinese location	Beijing	Shanghai	Shanghai	Beijing	Beijing	Shanghai
Number of Chinese-speaking employees in China	427	19	2	120	1	120

[a]As about the turnover, our respondent representing Company F, Ltd. mentioned the following statement: "Since we are the cost center and focus on R&D activity only, so number is sensitive and it is not allowed to be disclosed."

4.1 Company Profiles

According to Gersick (1988) and Pettigrew's approach (1990), Table 2 illustrates the most relevant pieces of information about our 6 companies.

4.2 Within and Cross-Case Analyses

We conducted qualitative and quantitative data analyses which will be illustrated in this section.

This part analyzes and discusses the open-ended questions about managers' understanding of "culture." Table 3 shows the results of managers' perceptions of psychic distance along each dimension. Language is the most perceived different dimension, followed by culture. Consistently with our theoretical background combining the extant literature on "culture" in international business (e.g., the CAGE model by Ghemawat 2001) and social psychology (Van Dijk 2008), we focus on managers' perceptions of culture (e.g., Hofstede 1980; Kogut and Singh 1988; Teerikangas and Very 2012). The use of language occurs in a specific cultural context (Van Dijk 2008; Gehmawat 2001). This is what our managers confirm in their answers. The figures appearing in the right column are the mean values between the replies about (1) degree of perceived differences between home and host country ("differences") and (2) degree of impact that is perceived along each dimension on the business with the host country ("impact").

Each dimension was graded on a Likert scale based on 5 points. More specifically, managers were asked how much difference they perceive along each dimension between their respective home country (in Europe) and China. As about the criteria used for interpreting the mean values, we considered as "relevant" the dimensions equal or higher than 4 (cutoff point—language 4.19 and culture 4—in bold).

We based the open-ended question about culture on these results (Table 3) and conducted a qualitative analysis by adopting the critical discourse analysis approach (Fairclough 1992; Wodak 2001). Critical discourse analysis was developed in response to the earlier and narrow approaches on the micro-linguistic aspects of discourse, which

Table 3 Psychic distance model and relevance of the "cultural" dimension

Psychic distance dimensions	"Differences" and "Impact" (mean values)
Language	**4.19**
Culture	**4**
Geographical distance	3.71
Accepted business practices	3.56
Level of technological development	3.45
Business ethics	3.50
Political system	3.40
Level of education	3.38
Legal system	3.26
Level of economic development	3.21
Regulations	3.19
Logistics infrastructure	2.83

Adapted from Child et al. (2009)

neglected its more macro-social aspects. Its origins can be found in Michel Foucault's studies on power and discourse (Sinclair and Coulthard 1975; Potter and Wetherell 1987; Fairclough 1993). In this way, we connected the textual elements with the sociocultural dynamics (Dreyfus and Rabinow 1982). The idea behind is that sociocultural structures become manifest through discourse and social practices; hence, our approach is a theoretical and methodological attempt to combine two levels: textual production and sociocultural aspects.

The critical discourse analysis is based on the analysis of the textual parts, the language, the most recurring words, expressions, and topics provided by our respondents. After having identified these pieces of information, we gathered them under several categories of abstraction (Table 4) (Ahonen et al. 2011): "national culture," "human resource practices," "shared beliefs," "business behaviour," "shared language," "cognitive knowledge." We focused on two levels of analysis, textual and sociocultural. Our aim was to identify managers' implicit values and meanings of culture emerging from the answers and relate them to international business contexts. The analysis is based on Van Dijk's approach (2000), whose purpose is to comprehend how ideologies and values affect texts and discourses as well as to comprehend how they

Table 4 Most recurrent textual elements emerging from the open-ended questions

Company	Quoted textual elements	Categorization
A	*It depends on the characteristic of the group, of the people in the organization. It depends on the country, political environment. It covers many areas: behaviour, customs, religion, food, all kind of things, arts, philosophy.*	National culture Human resource practices
	How to manage employees	
	How to communicate with employees from different countries	
	How to select and hire people	
B	*A way of thinking and how you see or looks at things or at situations and the say you resolve or take decisions*	Business behavior/ business practices
	Language, translation	National culture
	Politics, business, social, relations, religion	National culture
	China's thought has been developing for more than four – plus thousand years	
C	*Culture is a heritage from the past for a community. It is transmitted from a generation to another and so on along time*	Shared beliefs
D	*Culture is a common way of thinking of a group of people it will be affected by the history they share in a remote or recent past. Big achievements and natural or manmade disasters will be part of it too. Besides, the education system and doctrines they have faced will shape their culture*	Shared beliefs
E	*Local habits and customs*	Shared beliefs
F	*The cultural aspect has several dimensions.*	Business behavior
	Different kind of cultures: product and production culture or quality, internationalization culture, strategic culture	
	Difficulties in the internationalization process, if not due to the size of the company, in terms of dimension and investment capabilities, are due to cultural issues, namely to the definition of culture (set of intellectual cognition skills acquired through studying and experience)	
	Knowledge, openness, experience, previous success	

help to reproduce ideologies and values in society. Accordingly, ideology is defined as a set of values and norms that are shared by a social group. The aim is to implement the sociocultural practices of that group and reach its objectives. For the purpose of this chapter, we left apart ideology and concentrate on values, which are part of the cultural concept by definition (e.g., Van Dijk 2008).

The critical discourse analysis enabled us to analyze the sub-elements contained in the concept of culture according to our managers. First, they provided their general idea of culture. Secondly, they expressed the relevant issues regarding their perceptions of culture applied to China. Thirdly, they specifically applied their meaning and knowledge in business contexts. Results show three main areas, namely (1) a general understanding of culture, (2) the meaning of culture applied to the Chinese environment (host country-focused meaning), and (3) the meaning of culture referred to international business behavior.

In Table 4, "national culture" is the most recurrent category. In Table 3, specific aspects regarding the Chinese market emerge, therefore proving a certain degree of attention to the characteristics of the host country in terms of "cognitive knowledge" and "shared beliefs/language." Company B reports some detailed examples: *I have multiples examples, in politics, business, social relations, so not be surprise to hear these situations and all kind of things from the travellers and businessman/businesswomen or politicians where they spend hours and hours talking with the Chinese and when they go back home to Europe all the problems start coming out because each part understood differently.*

The emphasis on information about China shows the relevance of the local aspects, the attention and orientation to the host country, understanding and awareness of the crucial role played by culture in doing business in China ("business behaviour," "national culture," "shared beliefs"). The list in Table 5 (company F) illustrates the peculiar issues which usually come into play when dealing with the Chinese market (e.g., finding partners, management styles) and shows the local-context-oriented approach, for example, contextual intelligence, the opposite what social psychologists call "ethnocentric view"[10] (Sumner 1906). Another example is provided in Table 4 On the one hand, knowing the foreign market in terms of experience plays an essential role ("business

Table 5 "Chinese-culture" and "localization" textual elements emerging from the open-ended questions

Company	Quoted textual elements	Categorization
A	*Hiring local people*	Human resource practices
	Having local colleagues	
B	*China's culture is very far apart from our Greco-Judeo-Christian culture way of thinking – also language, which is not Indo-European language*	National culture, Shared beliefs/ language
	So in this culture the concepts are also different for instance, it's not the same the concept "Politics"-coming as you know from Greece, and "Politics" in Chinese language the semantics' translation is completely different.	National culture, Shared beliefs/ language
E	*Culture is one of the key points of success*	National culture
	In China culture is an extra dimension	National culture
	Chinese are proud people and they have respect for the culture and will always handle in this way especially in business with foreigners. This give them a comfortable feeling	National culture
	The numbers 8 and 9 means good luck and good life, next to the fact that they are used in feng shui, especially in the South of China. And also a small Buddha in the office can mean a lot, but we Westerners, we never think about it.	National culture, business behavior, shared beliefs
F	*Attention to diverse values, models of behaviour, awareness of the cultural gap and different business and management practices*	Business behavior
	Open issues regarding China: *1. Protection of intellectual property* *2. Finding reliable business partners* *3. Cultural gap and different management style* *4. Capacity to receive and benefit from Technology Transfer* *5. Financing opportunities for innovative ventures* *6. R&D institutions not fully open or prepared to cooperate with firms* *7. Clear policy direction information in specific high-tech sectors*	National culture
	Italian companies in China have always focused on the culture and/or quality of the product and of production. They exploited the national brand image, marketing strategies and international as well as distribution channels.	National culture

behavior"). On the other hand, drawing attention to the characteristics of the managers' home country emerged, especially regarding attitudes.

The replies to the open-ended question show how subjective and different are managers' understanding of the culture. They attribute to the cultural dimension a specific nuance and role. This determines their approach to their partners in the host country. They seem to attribute to culture a different role depending on which step of the internationalization process they face: the pre- or the post-market entry phase. Our respondents confirmed how much international business choices and processes are affected by culture and that their awareness and sensitiveness enable them to adopt a proactive attitude in overcoming culture-related issues in international business contexts.

From the questionnaire, we extracted and focused on those questions regarding the cultural dimension (Table 7):

As about investment decisions in the pre-market entry period, results show that European companies do not perceive culture as a major obstacle (question n. 2.3.3). In this context, access to local market, the presence of local business partners, logistical reasons, and local connections are ranked among the most important drivers. However, culture is a key dimension for European investors in terms of *non-regulatory* obstacles, regardless of the time collocation—pre- or post-entry phase. Among the options for replying to question n. 2.13, "cultural differences" is followed by "unfamiliarity of Chinese employees with Western style management." These features can be considered as perceptions of distance.

The relevance of culture as a dimension is further confirmed in the answers to questions n. 3.1 and 3.2. These questions are about the psychic distance model elaborated by Child et al. (2009) (Table 3). As first, our managers were asked to grade the difference that they perceive[11] between home country and host country along each of the 12 dimensions (question n. 3.1). Secondly, they were asked to grade the impact that each dimension has on their business with the target country (question n. 3.2).

Questions n. 2.19 and n. 2.20 are about investments in China and the relevance of culture and language. Culture was the most important dimension in the pre-market entry period. Most managers rely on

Chinese-speaking employees in their business unit in China (question n. 2.21 and 2.22).

To summarize our main findings, first of all, language and culture are the most relevant dimensions within the psychic distance model (Child et al. 2009). Secondly, according to the critical discourse analysis and to the categorization of managers' replies, not only language is relevant within the cultural dimension, but also business practices. This is consistent with the psychic distance dimensions ("accepted business practices"). Results show that managers define "culture" by distinguishing between two areas: general meaning and business-oriented meaning. The first one is related to shared values and principles, while the second one includes pragmatic elements, such as the use of language and business practices. Thirdly, replies show managers' "host bound" perception of identity, in other words, how they perceive China. In terms of "host bound" culture, when choosing a location in China, European managers seem not to consider the relevance of intra-China differences. Host-bound cultural perceptions may affect the business practices implemented by the company. Accordingly, those practices may be more "home country" oriented (e.g., ethnocentric view) or "host country" oriented (e.g., cultural competence or intelligence). Fourthly, from the open-ended questions, we can derive that cultural perceptions seem to be related to the phase of the internationalization process: pre- and post-market entry. Managers seem to realize about intra-China differences in the post-market entry.

A first observation from our main findings and the literature suggests that the cultural dimension, including language, affect a third dimension, that is the national one (Mantovani 2004; Brannen and Thomas 2010). Jimenéz et al. (2004) confirm that at national level common culture, customs and traditions, common language, common ancestry, and common history are related to the "cultural" conception of nation. In Tables 4, 5, and 6, we can see how our managers confirm the correlation between their perceptions of national culture and language.

Next to language and history, the ethno-cultural components of national identification include common culture, customs, and traditions. Child et al. (2002: 41) mention "home-bound identity" referred to those managers in the host country that are bounded to their home country. In the host country, the presence of respective ethnic groups mitigates the alienation, hence the perception of distance.

As about "host bound" perceptions of identity, European managers do not seem to make any differences when choosing a location within China. They seem to become aware of intra-China differences and perceive them after the market entry (Table 7, questions 3.1 and 3.2). Language and culture are considered among the five most important items for national identification and identity perceptions (Table 3, companies: B and F; Table 4, company F—"cognitive knowledge," "shared beliefs/language") (Jiménez et al. 2004; Eurobarometer surveys 2017). This leads to the following proposition regarding host-bound perceptions of culture and the differentiation between the pre- and the post-market entry phase in terms of perceptions:

Proposition no. 1:

European managers have lower awareness of culture in the pre-entry period than in post-entry period.

Before entering the market, European managers seem to relate the Chinese language and culture as nationally homogeneous, not considering regional differences within the country. After the market entry, they realize the intra-China differences thanks to the relevance that they attribute to the business practices (Tables 4, 5, and 6):

Proposition no. 2:

European managers have lower awareness of intra-China cultural differences in the pre-entry period than in the post-entry period.

As about host country, the answers to question 2.3.3 and the feedbacks illustrated in Tables 2, 3, and 4 confirm that awareness of intra-China differences seems to be acquired in the post-market entry period. In the pre-market entry period, managers seem to associate "one language" to "one culture." Chinese language stems from the same root throughout the country, despite regional language differences. Cultural dynamics are strongly related to linguistic structures, and the linguistic forms are inherited from one's own culture (e.g., Tables 4 and 5, "shared

Table 6 Culture-bound textual elements applied to international business emerging from the open-ended questions

Company	Quoted textual elements	Categorization
A	*In doing business in different countries cultural differences play an important role, especially regarding how to manage employees, how to communicate.*	Human resource practices
F	*In international projects and relations, we refer to culture as knowledge of (or attention to) cultural differences related to the target markets*	Cognitive knowledge
	The controversial issues of knowledge, openness, attention to diverse values, models of behaviour emerge when approaching new international markets	Cognitive knowledge/ business practices
	A recurring problem is referred to those companies which act on the basis of their previous successful experience and regardless the market they are going to approach. In other words, they approach the foreign markets by applying almost indistinctively their standard model	Business behavior/business practices

beliefs" and "shared language") (Hurford 1989). However, "business practices" is crucial in the post-market entry since it raises awareness of the regional differences intra-China.

Cultural and language factors are second to such drivers as access to regional markets, presence of a local business partner, logistical reasons, local connections, and availability of skilled labor (question n. 2.13). This may lead to the following consideration: Before entering the Chinese market, European investors have a general host-bound perception of identity and seem to underestimate intra-China cultural differences. Whereas in the post-market entry period, they interface locally and acquire a deeper intra-China awareness of differences and knowledge of different business practices. Table 3 (companies A and E) and Table 4 (companies A and F) confirm that after their experience in China, they acquired a better command of "human resource practices" (Tables 2 and 3).

Before entering China, European managers do not seem to take into account the local perspective; they seem to look at China as a

Table 7 Relevant questions about our unit of analysis - the role of cultural perceptions

	Questions	Reply items	Results
2.3.3	Reason for choosing a specific Province within China?	• Access to local market • presence of a local business partner • Availability/acquisition of key technologies and brands • Availability of skilled labor • Low labor cost • Tax regime/free tax zone/technology parks/special economic zone • Incentives and supportive policies • Logistical reasons • Cultural and language factors (Rank from 1 to 5, where 1 means not relevant, 5 means very important)	Results show that the culture and language are not considered important when choosing a certain location in China. (pre-entry period operations)
2.13	Did you encounter any of the following *non-regulatory* obstacles (operating, market and infrastructure difficulties) when investing in China?	• Cultural differences • Unfamiliarity of Chinese employees with Western style management • Hiring and maintaining local people • Managing local employees • Cost of personnel and other resources • Currency risk • Problems understanding the Chinese environment/market • General negative perception of European investment • Lack of suitable schooling facilities for children • Lack of expatriate community • Lack of awareness of the importance of environmental protection (Rank from 1 to 5, where 1 means not relevant, 5 means very important)	Cultural differences are key barriers to investments in China in terms of *non-regulatory* obstacles. Unfamiliarity of Chinese employees with Western style management is considered as the second most important *non-regulatory* obstacle

(continued)

Table 7 (continued)

	Questions	Reply items	Results
2.19	How important is the knowledge of the Chinese culture when investing in China?	1 2 3 4 5 (Rank from 1 to 5, where 1 means not relevant, 5 means very important)	Outcomes show the preponderance of the cultural dimension over language when investing in China (pre-entry period).
2.20	How important is the knowledge of the Chinese language when investing in China?		
2.21	Do you have Chinese-speaking employees in your Chinese firm?	Yes/no	Two companies only do not rely on Chinese-speaking employees in their Chinese firms (local workforce)[b]
2.22	Please indicate the number of Chinese-speaking employees in your Chinese firm.	(see Table 2)	
3.1	Evaluate the following dimensions, in terms of the *degree of difference between home country and host country*	• Geographical distance • Culture • Language • Level of education	Language—as a dimension of psychic distance—appears to be the most important one in the management of investment in China (post-entry period). Culture is the second most important dimension. These results report the sum of the mean values of both questions n. 3.1 and 3.2 (Table 3)
3.2	Evaluate the following features, in terms of to what extent each dimension *impacts on your business with the host country*.	• level of technological development • Level of economic development • Logistics infrastructure • Political system • Legal system • Regulations • Accepted business practices • Business ethics (Using a scale of 1 to 5, where: 1 = "no real difference"/"does not impact on my business at all" 5 = "very great difference"/"impacts on my business very much")	

[b]Question 2.22 enables us to identify the size of our companies and the position and roles covered by the Chinese-speaking employees in 20 out of 22 European companies investing in China we have been investigating. Despite the fact that this multiple case study includes 6 companies, our sample is an attempt to include a variety of company types in terms of size, core business, Chinese, and headquarter location

homogeneous entity with non-relevant intra-country differences. However, China is rich in regional cultural differences (e.g., Hyeon Jeong et al. 2010).

5 Conclusion

In order to be culturally successful in the target country, integration of the two cultures is necessary as well as knowledge and awareness of the cultural differences ("cognitive knowledge"), not only at national level but also at regional and firm level (e.g., location or area of the company, management and business practices, composition of the company team and company culture). Moreover, decision making may rely on tailoring the firm's model and practices to the host country context rather than relying 100% on previous achievements or prior experience (i.e., target-oriented sensitiveness, cultural sensitivity) (Johnson et al. 2006; Earley 2002; Khanna 2014; Thompson 2002).

We can recall the concepts developed by international business scholars over the years, such as "cultural competence," "cultural knowledge," "cultural sensitivity," "cultural intelligence," and "contextual intelligence." They are considered key ingredients to build bridges between home country and host country (Thompson 2002; Earley 2002; Earley and Ang 2003; Earley and Mosakowski 2004; Johnson et al. 2006; Khanna 2014). For example, cultural intelligence reflects individuals' capability to adapt when interacting with other individuals from different cultural areas. It is about how to learn and implement cognitive skills that allow to function effectively in a new culture, the motivational boost to adapt to a different environment and the ability to engage in adaptive behaviors (Earley and Ang 2003). Along with Gertsen's "cultural competence" (1990), the literature offers other examples in terms of competences, such as "global" and "transnational" competence (Adler and Bartholomew 1992; Adler et al. 1987).

This chapter aimed at analyzing the role of culture in European entry decisions in China. By adopting an international business perspective, we conclude that culture, including language, is the most important dimension within the concept of psychic distance. Relevant outcomes show that when investing in China, European managers are more aware of cultural differences within China in the post-entry rather than in the pre-entry period. This suggests that we may refer to "cultural experience," in terms of presence of the company over time in the foreign environment, rather than referring to *ex ante* cultural differences at national level.

Managers attribute to the cultural dimension a specific nuance and role. The internationalization phase seems to affect their cultural perceptions depending on the pre- and the post-market entry period. Furthermore, findings showed how subjective and different are managers' understanding of the culture.

As about location choices in the pre-market entry period, results show that European companies do not perceive culture as a major obstacle.

Next to language and culture, which resulted to be the most relevant dimensions within the psychic distance model, business practices and *non-regulatory obstacles* play a crucial role in raising managers' awareness on intra-China differences in the post-market entry.

Furthermore, "culture" is defined by distinguishing between two areas: a general meaning and a business-oriented meaning. The first one is related to shared values and principles, while the second one includes pragmatic elements, such as the use of language and business practices.

Culture, language, and business practices seem to determine "host bound" perceptions, in other words, how managers perceive China. When choosing a location in China, European managers seem not to consider the cultural dimension. They realize the relevance of intra-China differences in the post-market entry, when experiencing the local business practices and other non-regulatory obstacles. Thus, cultural perceptions seem to be related to the phase of the internationalization process: pre- and post-market entry.

The analytical generalization out of our multiple case study is limited to a specific industry and to specific home and target economic contexts. Therefore, testing the propositions of this study in a wider population of enterprises, industries, and areas could be recommended for future research.

Notes

1. "Language,“ culture," "level of education," "level of economic development," "level of technological development," "logistical infrastructure," "political system," "legal system," "regulations," "accepted business practices," "business ethics" (Child et al. 2009).
2. The EU-funded project is POREEN—*Partnering Opportunities between Europe and China in the Renewable Energies and Environmental iNdustries*. With its multidisciplinary approach, it gathers legal experts, engineers, and economist. The aim is to investigate a number of aspects of Chinese and Europe integration in the environmental and green tech sectors. (1) "This project is funded by the European Union under the Marie Curie Action's IRSES." (2) "This publication does not necessarily reflect the opinion of the EU" [When relevant]. The research leading to these results has received funding from the People Programme (Marie Curie Actions) of the European Union's Seventh Framework Programme FP7/2007–2013/under REA grant agreement n° 318908.
3. There is no consensus in the definition of green, probably due to the broadness of products and services, including consultancy services in the green tech industry, next to the fact that the sector is continuously being updated following the steady development of what is green and what is not green (Eurostat 2009; Salvatelli, 2014).
4. The complete questionnaire is available online: http://poll.econ.univpm.it//index.php?sid=56367andlang=en.
5. These three areas correspond to the areas covered by the EU project mentioned in the introductory part of this chapter.
6. European Chamber of Commerce, Handelskammer Deutschland—The German Chamber Network, GIZ—Deutsche Gesellschaft für die Internationale Zusammenarbeit—the German government association for international cooperation, EU SME Center, and Helpdesk China, etc.
7. The records account for 396 pages of material and a mean of 100–150 e-mail exchanges with each respondent.
8. For example, Euraxess Link China, Institute of Energy, Environment and Economy, Tsinghua University.
9. The researchers are affiliated to the Department of political sciences, communication, and international relations and Department of economics and law, University of Macerata, Italy.

10. "A differentiation arises between ourselves, the we-group, or in-group, and everybody else, or the others-groups, out-groups. The insiders in a we-group are in a relation of peace, order, law government, and industry, to each other...Ethnocentrism is the technical name of this view of things in which one's own group is the centre of everything, and all others are scaled and rated with references to it...Each group nourishes its own pride and vanity, boasts itself superior, exalts its own divinities, and looks with contempt on outsiders" (Sumner 1906: 12–13).
11. On a Likert scale based on 5 points.

References

Adler, N. J., & Bartholomew, S. (1992). Academic and professional communities of discourse: Generating knowledge on transnational human resource management. *Journal of International Business Studies, 2*(3), 551–569.
Adler, N. J., Graham, J. L., & Schwarz Gherke, T. (1987). Business negotiations in Canada, Mexico, and the United States. *Journal of Business Research, 15*(5), 411–429.
Ahonen, P., Tienari, J., & Vaara, E. (2011). There is no alternative" – or is there? A critical case study approach for international business research. In R. Piekkari & C. Welch (Eds.), *Rethinking the case study in international business research* (pp. 85–106). Cheltenham: Edward Elgar.
Aiwa, M., & Yang, C. (2010). Green credit, green stimulus, green revolution? China's mobilization of banks for environmental cleanup. *The Journal of Environment and Development, 19*(2), 119–144.
Ambos, B., & Håkanson, L. (2014). The concept of distance in international management research. *Journal of International Management, 20*(1), 1–7.
Anolli, L. (2004). *Psicologia della cultura.* Bologna: Il Mulino.
Barkema, H. G., Bell, J. H. J., & Pennings, J. M. (1996). Foreign entry, cultural barriers, and learning. *Strategic Management Journal, 17*(2), 151–166.
Baerveldt, C., & Voestermans, P. (2005). Culture, emotions, and the normative structure of reality. *Theory and Psychology, 15*(4), 449–473.
Benito, G., & Gripsrud, G. (1992). The expansion of Foreign direct investment: Discrete rational location choices or a cultural learning process? *Journal of International Business Studies, 23*(3), 461–476.
Billing, M. (1996). *Discutere e pensare. Un approccio retorico alla psicologia sociale.* Milano: Cortina.

Bourgeois, L., & Eisenhardt, K. (1988). Strategic decision processes in high velocity environments: Four cases in the microcomputer industry. *Management Science, 34*, 816–835.

Brannen, M. Y., & Thomas, D. C. (2010). Bicultural individuals in organizations: Implications and opportunity. *International Journal of Cross Cultural Management, 10*(1), 5–16.

Brewer, M. B. (2003). *Intergroup relations*. Berkshire: Free University Press.

Brewer, P. (2007). Psychic distance and Australian export market selection. *Australian Journal of Management, 32*(1), 73–94.

Brewer, P., & Venaik, S. (2011). Individualism–collectivism in Hofstede and GLOBE. *Journal of International Business Studies, 42*(3), 436–445.

Brouthers, K. D., & Brouthers, L. E. (2000). Acquisition or greenfield startup? Institutional, cultural and transaction cost influences. *Strategic Management Journal, 21*(1), 89–97.

Carson, S. (1974). International transmission of information and the business firm. *The Annals of the American Academy of Political and Social Science, 412*(1), 55–63.

Cattaneo, M. (2014). Elogio alla diversità. Un ambiente di ricerca eterogeneo aiuta la creatività. *Le Scienze (Italian version of Scientific American), 556*, 9–9.

Cheng, Y. -M. (2006). Determinants of FDI mode choice: Acquisition, brownfield, and greenfield entry in foreign markets. *Canadian Journal of Administrative Sciences Revue, 23*(3), 202–220.

Child, J., Ng, S. H., & Wong, C. (2002). Psychic distance and internationalization: Evidence from Hong Kong firms. *International Studies of Management and Organization, 32*(1), 36–56.

Child, J., Rodrigues, S. B., & Frynas, J. G. (2009). Psychic distance, its impact and coping modes: Interpretations of SMEs decision-makers. *Management International Review, 49*(2), 199–224.

Cole, M. (1996). *Cutural psychology. A once and future discipline*. Cambridge, Mass: The Belknap Press of Harvard University Press.

Deng, L. (1997). Understanding Japanese direct investment in China (1985–1993): An intercultural analysis. *American Journal of Economics and Sociology, 56*(1), 115–127.

Dow, D. (2000). A note on psychological distance and export market selection. *Journal of International Marketing, 8*(1), 51–64.

Dow, D., & Karunaratna, A. (2006). Developing a multidimensional instrument to measure psychic distance stimuli. *Journal of International Business Studies, 37*(5), 578–602.

Dreyfus, H. L., & Rabinow, P. (1982). *Michel foucault: Beyond structuralism and hermeneutics*. Brighton, Harvester, Chapter 4.

Earley, P. C. (2002). Redefining interactions across cultures and organizations: Moving forward with cultural intelligence. *Research in Organizational Behavior, 24,* 271–299.

Earley, P. C., & Ang, S. (2003). *Cultural intelligence: Individual interactions across cultures*. Stanford, CA: Stanford Business Books.

Earley, C. P., & Mosakowski, E. (2004). Cultural intelligence. *Harvard Business Review, 82*(10), 139–146.

Eisenhardt, K. M. (1989). Building theories from case study research. *Academy of Management Review, 14,* 532–550.

Eurobarometer surveys, public opinion. Available at http://ec.europa.eu/public_opinion/index_en.htm, Accessed Apr 2017.

Eurostat (2009). The environmental goods and service sector—a data collection handbook. Eurostat methodologies and Working Chapters, Luxembourg.

Evans, J., Treadgold, A., & Mavondo, F. T. (2000). Psychic distance and the performance of international retailers. A suggested theoretical framework. *International Marketing Review, 17*(4/5), 373–391.

Fairclough, N. (1992). *Discourse and social change* (Vol. 73). Cambridge: Polity Press.

Fairclough, N. (1993). Critical discourse analysis and the marketization of public discourse: The universities. Discourse and Society, *4*(2), 133–168.

Forsgren, M. (2002). The concept of learning in the Uppsala internationalization process model: a critical review. *International Business Review, 11*(3), 257–277.

Gao, T. (2005). Foreign direct investment in China: How big are the roles of culture and geography? *Pacific Economic Review, 10*(2), 153–166.

Geertz, C. (1973). *The interpretation of cultures*. New York: London Basic Books.

Gersick, C. (1988). Time and transition in work teams: Toward a new model of group development. *Academy of Management Journal, 31,* 9–41.

Ghemawat, P. (2001). Distance still matters: The hard reality of global expansion. *Harvard Business Review, 79*(8), 137–147.

Håkanson, L., Ambos, B., Schuster, A. & Leicht-Deobald, U. (2016). The Psychology of psychic distance: Antecedents of asymmetric perceptions. *Journal of World Business, 51*(2), 308–318.

Harzing, A. W. (2003). The role of culture in entry-mode studies: From neglect to myopia? In J. L. C. Cheng & M. A. Hitt (Eds.), *Managing multinationals in a knowledge economy: Economics culture advances in international management, 15*, 75–127. Emerald Group: Bingley.

Hashim, F. (2012). Outward internationalization and FDI: Motives for Malaysian MNEs moving into China. *Review of Business & Finance Studies, 3*(2), 89–102.

Hofstede, G. (1980). *Culture's consequences: International differences in work-related values*. Beverly Hills, CA: Sage.

Hofstede, G. (1983). The cultural relativity of organizational practices and theories. *Journal of International Business Studies, 14*(2), 75–89.

Hofstede, G. (1993). Cultural constraints in management theories. *Academy of Management Executive, 7*(1), 81–94.

Hofstede, G. (1994). *Cultures and organizasions: Software of the mind*. London: HarperCollins.

Hong, M., & Chen, L. S. (2001). Quantitative and dynamic analysis of the OLI variables determining FDI in China. *Review of Urban and Regional Development Studies, 13*(2), 163–172.

House, R. J., Hanges, P. J., Javidan, M., Dorfman, P. W., & Gupta, V. (2004). *Culture, leadership, and organization: The GLOBE study of 62 societies*. Thousand Oaks: Sage Publications.

Huang, R., & Chen, D. (2015). Does environmental information disclosure benefit waste discharge reduction? Evidence from China. *Journal of Business Ethics, 129*(3), 535–552.

Hurford, J. R. (1989). Biological evolution of the Saussurean sign as a component of the language acquisition device. *Lingua, 77*, 187–222.

Hyeon Jeong, C., Byoungho, J., & Hira, C. (2010). An examination of regional differences in China by socio-cultural factors. *International Journal of Market Research, 5*(52), 611–631.

Jiang, F. (2006). The determinants of the effectiveness of foreign direct investment in China: An empirical study of joint and sole ventures. *International Journal of Management, 23*(4), 891–908.

Jiménez, A. M., Górniak, J. J., Kosic, A., Kiss, P., & Kandulla, M. (2004). European and national identities in EU's old and new member states: Ethnic, civic, instrumental and symbolic components. In *European Integration online Chapters (EIoP)*, (Vol. 8, No. 11).

Johanson, J., & Wiedersheim-Paul, F. (1975). The internationalization of the firm—four Swedish cases. *Journal of Management Studies, 12*(3), 305–323.

Johanson, J., & Vahlne, J. E. (1977). The internationalization process of the firm: A model of knowledge development and increasing Foreign market commitments. *Journal of International Business Studies, 8*(1), 22–32.
Johnson, D., & Turner, C. (2004). *International business: Themes and issues in the modern global economy*. London: Routledge.
Johnson, J. P., Lenartowicz, T. & Apud, S. (2006). Cross-cultural competence in international business: Toward a definition and a model. *Journal of International Business Studies, 37*(4), 525–543.
Khanna, T. (2014). Contextual intelligence. *Harvard Business Review, 92*(9), 58–68.
Klein, S., & Roth, V. J. (1990). Determinants of export channel structure: The effects of experience and psychic distance reconsidered. *International Marketing Review, 7*(5), 27–38.
Kluckhohn, C., & Kroeber, A. (1963). *Culture: A critical review of concepts and definitions*. New York: Vintage Books.
Kogut, B., & Singh, H. (1988). The effect of national culture on the choice of entry mode. *Journal of International Business Studies, 19*(3), 411–432.
Kroeber, F. R., & Kluckhohn, F. L. (1952). *Culture: A critical review of concepts and definitions, Chapters of the Peabody Museum of American Archeology and Ethnology*. Cambridge, MA: Harvard University Press.
Krug, J. A., & Nigh, G. (1998). Top management departures in crossborder acquisitions: Governance issues in an international context. *Journal of International Management, 4*(4), 267–287.
Langer, K., & Watson, R. (2004). The greening of China's building industry. *China Business Review, 31*(6), 56–63.
Lees, S. (2003). *Global acquisitions: Strategic integration and the human factor*. New York: Palgrave MacMillian.
Lv, P., & Spigarelli, F. (2015). The integration of Chinese and European renewable energy markets: The role of Chinese foreign direct investments. *Energy Policy, 81*, 14–26.
Ma, Z., Yang, R., & Zhang, Y. (2008). Australia's direct investment in China: Trends and determinants. *Economic Papers, 27*(1), 70–86.
Makino, S., & Tsang, E. K. (2011). Historical ties and foreign direct investment: An exploratory study. *Journal of International Business Studies, 42*(4), 545–557.
Mantovani, G. (2004). *Intercultura: è possibile evitare le guerre culturali?* Bologna: Il Mulino.
Mantovani, G. (2006). Il difficile riconoscimento delle differenze. La necessità di una scelta tra due concezioni incompatibili della cultura. *Psicologia Sociale, 2*, 223–232.

Mantovani, G. (2007). Dalla psicologia culturale alla prospettiva interculturale. In B. Mazzara, (Ed.), *Prospettive di psicologia culturale*, 57–76. Roma: Carocci.

Morosini, P., Shane, S., & Singh, H. (1998). National cultural distance and crossborder acquisition performance. *Journal of International Business Studies, 29*(1), 137–158.

Nebus, J., & Chai, K. H. (2013). Putting the "psychic" back in psychic distance: Awareness, perceptions, and understanding as dimensions of psychic distance. *Journal of International Management, 20*(1), 8–24.

Olie, R. (1994). Shades of culture and institutions in international mergers. *Organization Studies, 15*(3), 381–405.

Ozawa, T. (1979). International investment and industrial structure: New theoretical implications from the Japanese experience. *Oxford Economic Papers, 31*(1), 72–92.

Patton, M. Q. (1990). *Qualitative evaluation and research methods*. Newbury Park: Sage.

Pettigrew, A. (1990). Longitudinal field research on change: Theory and practice. *Organization Science, 1*, 267–292.

Pew Charitable Trusts (Pew). (2011). Who's winning the clean energy race? 2010 Edition: G-20 Investment Powering Forward. http://www.pewenvironment.org/uploadedFiles/PEG/Publications/Report/G-20Report-LOWRes-FINAL.pdf. Accessed Apr 2017.

Pothukuchi, V., Damanpour, F., Choi, J., Chen, C. C., & Park, S. H. (2002). National and organizational culture differences and international joint venture performance. *Journal of International Business Studies, 33*(2), 243–265.

Potter, J., & Wetherell, M. (1987). *Discourse and social psychology: Beyond attitudes and behaviour*. London: Sage.

Powell, M., & Ansic, D. (1997). Gender differences in risk behaviour in financial decision-making: An experimental analysis. *Journal of economic psychology, 18*(6), 605–628.

Puthussery, P. N., Child, J., & Rodrigues, S. B. (2014). Psychic distance, its business impact and modes of coping: A study of British and Indian partner SMEs. *Management International Review, 54*, 1–29.

Reus, T. H., & Rottig, D. (2009). Meta-analyses of international joint venture performance determinants: Evidence for theory, Methodological artifacts and the unique context of China. *Management International Review, 49*(5), 607–640.

Rottig, D., Reus, T. H., & Tarba, S. Y. (2013). The impact of culture on mergers and acquisitions: A third of a century of research. In C. Cooper & S. Finkelstein (Eds.), *Advances in mergers and acquisitions*. Bingley: Emerald Group Publishing Limited.

Salavrakos, I. (2010). Business history and conflicting entrepreneurial culture and explanatory factors of success and failure of FDI in Chinese economy. *Studies in Economics and Finance, 27*(4), 276–298.

Salvatelli, F. (2014). *Defining green sectors: A pre-requisite to analyze China-Europe cooperation in the green industries* (Working paper [2281–5023]), c.MET-05 - Centro Interuniversitario di Economia Applicata alle Politiche per L'industria, lo Sviluppo locale e l'Internazionalizzazione.

Shenkar, O. (2001). Cultural distance revisited: Towards a more rigorous conceptualization and measurement of cultural differences. *Journal of International Business Studies, 32*(3), 519–535.

Sinclair, J., & Coulthard, R. M. (1975). *Toward an analysis of discourse*. Oxford: Oxford University Press.

Sousa, C. M., & Bradley, F. (2006). Cultural distance and psychic distance: two peas in a pod?. *Journal of International Marketing, 14*(1), 49–70.

Sousa, C. M., & Bradley, F. (2008). Cultural distance and psychic distance: Refinements in conceptualisation and measurement. *Journal of Marketing Management, 24*(5/6), 467–488.

Stahl, G. K., & Voigt, A. (2008). Do cultural differences matter in mergers and acquisitions? A tentative model and examination. *Organization Science, 19*(1), 160–176.

Stöttinger, B., & Schlegelmilch, B. B. (2000). Psychic distance: A concept past its due date? *International Marketing Review, 17*(2), 169–173.

Sumner, W. G. (1906). *Folksways*. New York: Ginn.

Teerikangas, S., & Very, P. (2012). Culture in mergers and acquisitions: A critical synthesis and steps forward. In D. Faulkner, S. Teerikangas, & R. J. Joseph (Eds.), *The handbook of mergers and acquisitions*. Oxford: Oxford University Press.

The World Bank and Development Research Center of the State Council, the People's Republic of China. (2013). *Seizing the opportunity of green development in China* (pp. 229–292). Available at: http://www.worldbank.org/content/dam/Worldbank/document/SR3–229-292.pdf/http://elibrary.worldbank.org/doi/abs/10.1596/9780821395455_CH03. Accessed Apr 2017.

Thompson, C. J. (2002). A re-inquiry on re-inquiries: A postmodern proposal for a critical-reflexive approach. *Journal of Consumer Research, 29*(2), 142–145.

Tihanyi, L., Griffith, D. A., & Russell, C. J. (2005). The effect of cultural distance on entry mode choice, international diversification, and MNE performance: A meta-analysis. *Journal of International Business Studies, 36,* 270–283.

Tsang, E. W. (1994). Human resource management problems in Sino-Foreign Joint Ventures. *International Journal of Manpower, 15*(9), 4–21.

Turner, J. C. (1975). Social comparison and social identity: Some prospects for intergroup behaviour. *European Journal of Social Psychology, 5,* 5–34.

Uhlenbruck, K. (2004). Developing acquired foreign subsidiaries: The experience of MNEs in transition economies. *Journal of International Business Studies, 35,* 109–123.

Vaccarini, K., & Pojaghi, B. (2015). *Capitalizing on cultural difference: A cross-disciplinary outlook from social psychology to international business.* (c.MET Working Papers 1508), *c.MET-05 - Centro Interuniversitario di Economia Applicata alle Politiche per L'industria, lo Sviluppo locale e l'Internazionalizzazione.* https://socionet.ru/publication.xml?h=repec:cme:wpaper:1507&l=en. Accessed Apr 2017.

Vaara, E. (2000). Constructions of cultural differences in post-merger change processes: A sensemaking perspective on Finnish-Swedish cases. *Management, 3*(3), 81–110.

Vaara, E., Tienari, J., & Säntti, R. (2003). The international match: Metaphors as vehicles of social identitybuilding in crossborder mergers. *Human Relations, 56*(4), 419–451.

Van Dijk, T. A. (2000). *Ideology and discourse a multidisciplinary introduction.* Barcelona: Pompeu Fabra University.

Van Dijk, T. A. (2008). *Context. Towards a multidisciplinary theory.* Cambridge: Cambridge University Press.

Veiga, J., Lubatkin, M., Calori, R., & Very, P. (2000). Measuring organizational culture clashes: A two-nation post-hoc analysis of a cultural compatibility index. *Human Relations, 53*(4), 539–557.

Villinger, R. (1996). Postacquisition managerial learning in Central East Europe (Special Issue on Managerial Learning in Transformation of Eastern Europe). *Organization Studies, 17*(2), 181–206.

Vygotskij, L. S. (1978). *Mind in society: The development of higher psychological processes.* Cambridge, MA: Harvard University Press.

Vygostkij, L. S. (1934). *Pensiero e linguaggio.* Bari, Laterza (1990).

Weber, Y. (1996). Corporate cultural fit and performance in mergers and acquisitions. *Human Relations, 49*(9), 1181–1202.
Wodak, R. (2001). *What CDA is About—a Summary of its History, Important Concepts and its Developments*, In R. Wodak & M. Meyer (Eds.), 1–13, Thousand Oaks, CA: Sage.
Yin, R. K. (1994). *Case study research: Design and methods* (2nd ed.). Thousand Oaks, CA: Sage.
Yin, R. K. (2003). *Case study research: Design and methods* (3rd ed.). Thousand Oaks, CA: Sage.
Yin, R. K. (2014). *Case study research: Design and methods* (5th ed.). Thousand Oaks, CA: Sage.
Yoshino, M. Y. (1976). *Japan's multinational enterprises*. Cambridge, MA: Harvard University Press.
Zihui, M., Ruilong, Y., & Zhang, Y. (2008). Australia's direct investment in China: Trends and determinants. *Economic Papers, 27*, 70–86.

5

Chinese FDI and Psychic Distance Perceptions on Regulations in the German Renewable Energy Sector

Abstract Countries are different on various dimensions such as culture, language, business practices, policy-making, and regulation. Research shows that distances on these dimensions between countries impact foreign direct investments (FDIs) flows. The higher the distances, the higher the difficulties for businesses. In this chapter, we analyze the perception of distances between China and Germany, by surveying Chinese managers who invested in Germany in the renewable energy (RE) sector. Our analysis refers to Child et al.'s measure of psychic distance (PD), which consists of 12 dimensions. The RE sector is young and highly dynamic. Regulations, policy-making, and business practices—all dimensions of the PD concept—are under permanent change, and this may lead to wrong perceptions, therefore to failures in FDI decisions. We use a five-company multiple case study and analyze if managers perceive distances on various dimensions, in particular regulation based, and if Chinese managers have correct perceptions

Reprinted from Vaccarini, K., Lattemann, C., Spigarelli, F. and Tavoletti, E. (2017), "Chinese FDI to Germany in the renewable energy sector: Pre- and post-entry psychic distance perceptions on regulations-related dimensions," *Energy Policy*, Vol. 101, pp. 723–732, Copyright (2017), with permission from Elsevier.

K. Vaccarini et al., *Cultural Distance in International Ventures*,
DOI 10.1007/978-3-319-62193-7_5

or "misperceptions." Further, we investigate if their perceptions change over time. Findings lead to recommendations for policy-making in the RE sector, for practitioners in the field of FDI to cope with issues of distances, and for international business (IB) scholars by showing that psychic distance should be complemented by a dynamic dimension.

Keywords Pre-entry · Post-entry · Managers' perceptions · Psychic distance dimensions · Culture · Language · Geographical distance · Level of education · Level of economic development · Level of technological development · Political system · Legal system · Regulations · Accepted business practices · Business ethics · Differences · Impact · FDI · China · Germany · Chinese investment to Germany · RE/renewable energy sector · International business · Policy-making

1 Introduction

Recent research in international business (IB) mentions psychic distance (PD) as a major factor impacting outward foreign direct investments (OFDIs), their determinants, and location choices (Beckerman 1956; Linnemann 1966; Gruber and Vernon 1970; Johanson and Wiedersheim-Paul 1975). Vaccarini et al. (2015) show that European managers' perceptions between their home country and China change over time, i.e., between before and after entering China. Our chapter will follow up on this observation and, in particular, will analyze if psychic distance perceptions of Chinese managers—pursuing FDI in the German renewable energy (RE) industry—will also change from pre-market entry to post-market entry with particular respect to regulation-related psychic distance dimensions (i.e., "political system," "legal system," and "regulations"). Many recent IB studies have been conducted on the relationship between psychic distance and FDI (e.g., Child et al. 2002; Brewer 2007; Child et al. 2009; Hashim 2012; Puthussery et al. 2014; Hertenstein et al. 2015). However, to the best of our knowledge, none of them focus on FDI from China to Germany. More specifically, this chapter focuses on the RE industry, because of the increasing importance of this industry in IB, and because the RE sector is young and highly dynamic. Hence, industry rules, laws, regulations, policy-making, and business practices are under permanent change which makes it difficult for managers to build correct perceptions of differences between countries.[1]

In recent years, the combination of the increasing environmental awareness in China and the economic recession in Europe has created a climate, which is increasingly conducive to Chinese OFDI in the RE industry (Lv and Spigarelli 2016). China has been devoting increasing attention to environmental issues and pollution reduction. A wide and comprehensive "green policy" has been embedded in the recent Chinese Five-Year Plans, and the national industry has grown in size and competitiveness. In Europe, since the recession in 2008, reduction in public spending has forced many governments to reduce public support in this sector. This impacts subsidized industries such as the RE and the green sector. As a result, European firms are repositioning and also targeting cooperation with foreign firms, mostly from emerging markets to find business opportunities (Lv and Spigarelli 2015).

Recent studies on the interactions between the European and the Chinese RE markets (Curran 2015; Lv and Spigarelli 2015, 2016) report that Europe has become an important destination for sales from Chinese global RE firms. Among them, Germany is one of the world largest investors in the RE sector and is a popular destination for Chinese OFDI (e.g., Lv and Spigarelli 2016). In general, the RE sector is highly affected by regulation. In particular, in Europe regulation in the RE underwent major changes over the past decade (Curran et al. 2016).

Our chapter analyzes how the dimensions of psychic distance influence Chinese OFDI to Germany in the RE sector. Building on Child et al.'s (2009) 12 dimensions of psychic distance, our study aims, firstly, at analyzing the importance of these dimensions in the internationalization process of firms and secondly, at deeper investigating to what extent managers' perceptions before and after a foreign market entry change over time. In doing so, we look at Chinese managers' perceptions of psychic distance between their home country and Germany in two points in time, i.e., before and after the foreign market entry. The analysis shows that a cluster of three regulation-related dimensions ("political system," "legal system," and "regulations") are most relevant for Chinese FDI to Germany in the RE sector out of the 12 dimensions identified by Child et al. (2009). This is not surprising, as regulation in the RE sector is high and underlies constant changes. Hence, we specifically focus on these dimensions and their dynamics over time.

The chapter makes several contributions to the existing literature. Firstly, by measuring and analyzing the differences between psychic distance perceptions in the pre-market entry and post-market entry stage (Child et al. 2002, 2009), we uncover a new perspective of the role of psychic distance on FDI with a focus on the RE sector and on regulation-specific dimensions. Secondly, we provide a more in-depth analysis on Child et al.'s (2009) 12 psychic distance dimensions and their impact on businesses. Thirdly, we conduct a sectorial analysis of Chinese FDI in Europe, consistently with Child et al. (2002) as well as Lv and Spigarelli (2016), who pinpoint the need for conducting industry-level analyses. This chapter proceeds as follows. We review the existing literature, identify theories, and present five case studies to derive propositions. The main findings will be discussed and conclusions will be drawn.

2 Background and Literature Review

This chapter is based on research from IB and psychology. Research in psychology shows that individuals, such as managers, tend to prefer familiar situations rather than unfamiliar ones (Powell and Ansic 1997). IB scholars have conducted studies on the concept of psychic distance, which implicitly captures this insight. It suggests that perceived differences between the home and host country's characteristics may generate uncertainties among managers and affect their decisions in the internationalization process (Child et al. 2009). As about perceptions, social psychology deals with three levels of analysis: individual-, interpersonal-, and group-level. In this research, we focus on the individual-level of managers' perceptions of psychic distance. Further, the social psychological perspective enables a comprehensive view of international business phenomena. The individual-level is related to the group-level through the act of categorization (Turner 1975). Individuals tend to group things together and to form categories in order to facilitate the information processing (Wilder 1978). "The act of categorizing a person into a social grouping automatically classifies that individual as a member of an ingroup [...] or outgroup [...]" (Brewer 2003: 5). As groups give a sense of social identity, individuals tend to enhance the status of social identity and provide an important source of self-esteem. Individuals tend to enhance the status of the group to which they belong to increase their self-image (Tajfel and Turner 1979). Once categories have been formed, the tendency for perceivers is to exaggerate the extent of differences between members of one category and another, resulting in an increase in perceived homogeneity within categories and distinctiveness (or distance) between categories (Tajfel and Wilkes 1963). In our research context, the perceived distinctiveness between one's own and another culture is the concept of "psychic distance" (PD).

Studies on people's perceptions are reflected in IB research and in the operationalization of psychic distance (e.g., Stöttinger and Schlegelmilch 1998). And as essentially "international management is management of distance" (Zaheer et al. 2012: 19), in the remainder of this chapter, we will incorporate the research on "perceptions" with the concept of "distance" in the context of Chinese OFDI to Germany in the RE sector.

2.1 The Concept of Distance

The concept of "distance" is a pivotal aspect in IB research. The first form of "distance" that was analyzed in IB was "geographic distance" and its impact on the decision-maker in firm's internationalization process (Linnemann 1966, Leamer 1974). Later concepts introduced economic (Berry et al. 2010), institutional (Xu and Shenkar 2002; Salomon and Wu 2012), cultural (Brouthers 2002), and other differences (Campbell et al. 2012) to IB researchers.

Initially, psychic distance was defined as a series of factors preventing or disturbing the corporate learning process and the understanding of foreign environments (e.g., Nordström and Vahlne 1994). Psychic distance was described as the sum of distance-creating factors, such as cultural, structural, and language differences, minus the sum of distance-bridging factors, such as knowledge or trial and error processes.

Commonalities (signals of similarity) between countries are distance-reducing factors whereas differences (signals of dissimilarity) are distance-augmenting ones. There is recognized evidence that managers perceive and consider commonalities between their home country and a potential internationalization target country. The higher their preference for selecting this particular target for their firm's first expansion abroad, the earlier they prefer to enter (Williams and Grégoire 2015).

The term "psychic distance" has been coined by Beckerman (1956) in his analysis of factors that explain trades and investments between countries. However, the concept has been a marginal one in IB research till the late 1970s when the first empirical work on psychic distance with reference to the internationalization process appeared (Johanson and Wiedersheim-Paul 1975; Johanson and Vahlne 1977). The concept's history, from the factual perspective of Nordic studies till the cognitive (Evans et al. 2000) and perceptual (Stöttinger and Schlegelmilch 2000) approaches, has been well described by Child et al. (2009) and more recently in a JIBS article by Williams and Grégoire (2015).

Even though factual "cultural distance" (Kogut and Singh 1988; Caprar et al. 2015) has been widely used in research (Sousa and Bradley 2006), research show that psychic distance is a better predictor for describing exporting activities than cultural distance (Dow 2000; Shenkar 2001, 2012). Since cognition plays a significant role in terms of managers' perceptions and understanding, the cognitive dimension is the core element of the psychic distance concept (Evans et al. 2000). Generally speaking, in IB, psychic distance implicitly captures insights from studies conducted in psychology (Powell and Ansics 1997).

Williams and Grégoire (2015) provide a valuable addition to this discussion. They differentiate between alignable differences (differences which might converge, such as common language or shared values) and non-alignable differences (e.g., non-shared values or principles which cannot be bridged). If managers perceive the difference as alignable, they tend to prefer low-commitment entry modes, because they see no necessity for high control. If managers perceive the differences as non-alignable, they prefer high-commitment modes of entry, such as FDI, to have more control over the situation. That implies that non-alignable perceived differences between Europe and China might induce Chinese managers to undertake FDI for entering a market (Williams and Grégoire 2015).

Managers are the core individuals in our study as they are the decision-makers in a company. Hence, they constitute our unit of investigation. The in-depth study of managers' perceptions derives from their crucial role as decision-makers, whose perceptions and skills in facing psychic distance determine the success, the performances, or the failure of the firm's internationalization process (Harzing 2003; Brewer 2007; Child et al. 2009; Hashim 2012).

Child et al. (2002, 2009) define psychic distance as the existing perceived distance between home country and host country in terms of the following characteristics: factual (Johanson and Wiedersheim-Paul 1975; Johanson and Vahlne 1977), cognitive (Evans et al. 2000), and perceptual (Stöttinger and Schlegelmilch 2000). Our analysis follows the approach of Child et al. (2009) by adopting the following 12 sub-dimensions of perceived psychic distance:

2.2 Chinese Firms Investing Abroad: Home and Host Country Factors

Chinese firms' international expansion has been examined from different viewpoints. Among them, particularly the analyses that base on home vs. host country-specific factors are helpful for our study. In fact, when looking simultaneously at home and host country factors, a certain idea of distance emerges. Rugman and Chang (2008) argue that emerging market multinational enterprises (MNEs) expand abroad largely on the strength of home country factors, such as access to resources and cheap labor. In later research, home country's "pull" and "push" factors are introduced into the discussion (Luo and Wang 2012; Wei and Alon 2010). In the case of China, international expansion is pushed by preferential policies and financial support provided by the Chinese government (Peng et al. 2008). Among push factors, some authors stress the necessity by Chinese companies to overcome domestic institutional voids (Luo and Tung 2007; Puri et al. 2015). Pull factors (i.e., host country-specific advantages) include the level of economic development (Buckley et al. 2007; Cheng and Ma 2008; Kolstad and Wiig 2012; Stoian 2013), market size, and specific endowments such as strategic assets, natural resources, or cheap labor (Buckley et al. 2007; Cheung and Qian 2009; Kolstad and Wiig 2012). Among host country factors, a specific attention has been drawn on institutions. Host institutional country-specific advantages (CSAs) include elements such as policy liberalization and openness to inward FDI (Buckley et al. 2007; Lau 2003; Lecraw 1977; Wells 1983; Zhou 2006). Lv and Spigarelli (2015, 2016) argue that a comprehensive view of country factors should include measures of distance, culture, language, and other non-economic factors such as business practices. They argue that low distance and differences could be considered as push factors for FDI. But in case of large differences, culture and language could also become a country-specific disadvantage.

In our chapter, we contextualize the concept of psychic distance by applying it to Chinese OFDI to Germany in the RE sector. As Child et al. (2009) mention, analyses of psychic distance in the context of IB need to take changes of psychic distance (dynamics) over time into consideration (Child et al. 2002). Consistently, Vaccarini et al. (2015) showed that perceptions change over time by describing two different stages of perceptions: the perceptions before actual experiences in the pre-market entry and after having concrete experiences in the post-market entry stage.

Given the described context, in our chapter, we focus on the following core research questions:

1. What is the importance of psychic distance for Chinese managers in the context of RE OFDI to Germany? and
2. To what extent do psychic distance perceptions of Chinese managers to the German market change from pre- to post-market entry in the RE industry?

Several issues, related to those questions, are addressed. Firstly, we consider the extent to which managers are aware of psychic distance. Secondly, we study whether they distinguish between the different dimensions of the construct with a focus on regulation-related psychic distance dimensions. Thirdly, we focus on the relevance that managers attribute to different components of psychic distance in terms of their possible impact on conducting business abroad. By addressing these questions, we contribute to a better understanding of how (Chinese) manager interpret and become aware of the psychic distance constituent dimensions. They may apply their interpretation to the management of the internationalization process of their firm in two stages, before and after entering the market. In this context, the relevance of the cognitive aspect of psychic distance emerges. Understanding how managers conduct their business at an international level means to focus on the way they perceive the situation in which they work (Child et al. 2009).

3 Methodology

We adopted a multiple case study research design based on Eisenhardt (1989, 2009) and Yin's (2003) methodology. A case study design is the most appropriate methodology because of the explorative nature of our research questions and enables us to generate propositions after conducting accurate within and cross-case analyses.

According to the German Federal Foreign Office, there are currently about 900 Chinese companies operating in Germany (German Federal Foreign Office 2015). Lv and Spigarelli (2015) mapped 135 Chinese firms in RE sectors in Europe, by using a dataset from 2004 to 2013, 40% of which are located in Germany. We use a convenience sample of this population consisting of five companies headquartered in China which have recently (within the past 10 years) entered the German RE market through FDI. The Chinese Chamber of Commerce in Berlin, a private consultancy company[2] and the exhibitors' database of the annual international fair on RE, held in Munich[3] helped us to identify these five companies.

Table 1 Child et al.'s dimensions of PD

Geographical Distance	Culture	Language
Level of Education	Level of Technological development	Level of Economic development
Logistical Infrastructure	Political System	Legal System
Regulations	Accepted Business Practices	Business Ethics

Adapted from Child et al. (2009)

We followed a triangulation approach (Yin 2003) by collecting data from interviews and various other resources, such as companies' Internet Web sites and annual reports, other publicly available information from newspapers and publications such as existing case studies (Table 1).

Our data collection took place in Spring/Summer 2015 in Germany, based on a questionnaire[4] and in Fall/Winter 2015 by submitting a round of follow-up questions based on the first results. At this later stage, we first asked the managers whether they were in the company before the setting up of the investment in Germany. Secondly, we asked them to emphasize on regulation-related psychic distance dimensions since this dimension underwent significant variations over time in terms of perceptions. By replying to our research questions, we first articulated the relevance of every psychic distance constituent dimension, building on Child et al. (2009) 12-item model. Secondly, we discover the extent to which managers' psychic distance perceptions differ between the pre- and post-market entry stages. The questionnaire is composed of Likert-scale and open-ended questions to get a comprehensive overview of the information provided by the respondents. In this way, we combine quantitative and qualitative methods of analyses. The Likert-scale questions served to ascribe quantitative values to our qualitative data regarding perceptions of differences and impact along the 12 dimensions. "Perceptions of differences" is defined by the extent to which managers perceive each psychic distance dimension as different between their home country and host country. "Perceptions of impact" is referred to what extent each psychic distance dimension affects the business with the host country. The questionnaire is structured in five sections as follows (Table 2):

Table 2 Sections and content of the questionnaire

Section 1	General information about respondents
Section 2	Information about the Chinese headquarter, the investment in Germany, and the entry mode choice
Section 3	Managers' PD perceptions before entering a market (Child et al.'s 2009 12-item list)
Section 4	Managers' PD perceptions after entering a market (the 12-item list repeats)
Section 5	Open-ended question regarding the managers' understanding of "culture"

Managers filled out the questionnaire in which they were asked to recollect their perceptions of differences and impact in two points in time: the pre-market entry period (Sect. 3, Table 2) and the post-market entry period (Sect. 4, Table 2). The questionnaire (Table 2) was answered by e-mail (one company out of five), direct contact via phone calls (three companies), and by meeting the respondent face-to-face (one company). The answers were written down on the printed hard copy questionnaires by the interviewer. Subsequently, they were scanned and sent to the respective respondents via e-mail to double check the accuracy of the replies.

For the purpose of our chapter, we focus primarily on the first four sections of the questionnaire (Table 2). Section 5, containing the open-ended questions, is of secondary importance. In order to analyze the data of the fifth section, we borrowed the critical discourse analysis from the discipline area of sociolinguistics (CDA, Fairclough 1993; Van Dijk 2000) and applied it to the texts of the answers. The purpose of the CDA is to go through the written answers and identify the most recurrent pieces of information, topics, and textual expressions (Ahonen et al. 2011). In our case, we aimed at identifying which psychic distance dimensions were most relevant to our respondents. We then proceeded with a "static" analysis and a "dynamic" analysis of our results. The static analysis shows the relevance of the psychic distance dimensions both in terms of perceived differences and impact. The analysis of the "dynamics" in psychic distance enables us to detect to what extent perceptions of differences and impact change over time. At last, the follow-up questions were based on the first results showing the relevance of eight dimensions (which overcame the threshold of 3.33 that we established for the analysis in the following section): "regulations," "legal system," "political system," and "culture" (regulation-cluster, Table 6, decreasing order).

4 Data, Analyses, and Propositions

The Chinese companies in our sample entered Germany between 2008 and 2014 (Table 3). Our respondents are all Chinese managers. They come from different regions in China and cover the following positions: manager's assistant, general manager, director of global sales, marketing manager, and general manager. Three out of five have neither previous work nor investment experience or have studied abroad (cf. Table 7).

4.1 Within-Case Analysis

This section provides the description of the five companies (Table 3) followed by an in-depth analysis.

Company A: The headquarter of the company is located in Beijing and established its wholly owned subsidiary in Hamburg in 2012. It is a service and distribution company in RE, specifically solar photovoltaic and solar thermal energy. The main reasons for choosing Germany are the following: access to local market, availability and acquisition of key technologies and brands, finally, incentives and supportive policies. Existing contacts and political factors were the main motives of the firm entry mode choice. The manager neither had any previous work experience in Germany nor had he studied or invested abroad.

Company B: headquartered in Ningbo, settled its wholly owned subsidiary in Nuremberg in 2011. The company operates in the RE business, service and distribution of solar technology. Political and economic factors were the main entry mode determinants, while access to local market and incentives and supportive policies were the most relevant

Table 3 Company profiles

Investment in Germany	Company A	Company B	Company C	Company D	Company E
German location	Hamburg	Nürnberg	Frankfurt am Main	Willich	Bremen
Chinese headquarter	Beijing	Ningbo	Wuxi	Nanjing	Shenzhen
Year of establishment in Germany	2012	2011	2008	2005	2014
Respondents' position and nationality	General Manager, Chinese	Management Assistant and Admin, Chinese	Director of Global Sales, Chinese	Marketing Manager, Chinese	General Manager, Chinese
FDI entry mode	Wholly owned subsidiary	Wholly owned subsidiary	Wholly owned subsidiary	Wholly owned subsidiary	Wholly owned subsidiary
Turnover in China (USD)	3,000,000	50,000,000	22,000,000	28,000,000	55,000
Core business	RE. Service and distribution	RE. Service and distribution	RE. Service and distribution	RE, Electric power infrastructure. R&D and Marketing services	RE, Electric power infrastructure, Green building, Efficient processing, optimized design, sustainable materials, monitoring systems, Marketing services

motives for choosing Germany. The interviewed manager in charge had not previously worked in Germany or studied abroad. This is his first experience with investments abroad.

Company C: headquartered in Wuxi, entered the German market in 2008 by establishing its wholly owned subsidiary in Frankfurt/Main. RE—photovoltaic panels—service and distribution are the key areas of the company. Germany was mainly chosen for the following motives: access to local market, presence of a local business partner. The manager in charge had neither worked in Germany previously nor studied abroad. However, he is already experienced with foreign investments.

Company D: is based in Nanjing and established its wholly owned subsidiary in Willich in 2005 attracted by legal factors and an easy access to the local market, presence of local business partners and existing connections. The core business of the company in Germany is RE—solar products and solutions, research and development, and marketing services. The manager neither has previous work experiences in Germany nor has studied abroad. This is also his first foreign investment.

Company E: located in Shenzhen and invested in Germany, Bremen, because of existing local business partners, key technologies, relevant brands, and for logistical reasons. The parent company is a manufacturer of measuring instruments and technologies. Economic reasons were the most important motives for choosing a wholly owned subsidiary entry mode. The manager has worked and studied in Germany before the company's investment. However, he does not have any previous experience with investments abroad. We conducted (1) a static analysis by focusing on two points in time, the pre- and post-market entry, and (2) an analysis of the dynamics in order to reveal the changes in perceptions before and after entering the market. The results of both analyses are shown in Table 4

Table 4 Companies' PD perceptions

Companies (represented by our managers)	Difference			Impact		
	Static analysis		Dynamic analysis	Static analysis		Dynamic analysis
	Pre-entry	Post-entry	Changes (%)	Pre-entry	Post-entry	Changes (%)
Company A	**4**	**4.08**	+0.08 (+2%)	**4**	**4.08**	+0.08 (+2%)
Company B	3.08	2.5	**−0.58 (−18.83%)**	**4.16**	**3.83**	**−0.33 (−7.93%)**
Company C	**3.33**	2.41	**−0.92 (−27.63%)**	2.91	2	**−0.91 (−31.27%)**
Company D	**4.25**	**4.08**	−0.17 (−4%)	**4.25**	**4.25**	0
Company E	**3.83**	**3.83**	0	**3.41**	**3.41**	0

and Table 5. We came up with the following rubric to interpret the data:

1. In the static analysis, the dimension is considered *relevant* if the corresponding Likert-scale value (ranging from strongly agree (5) to not agree at all (1)) equals or overcomes 3.33 points, since this value is slightly above the midpoint of the Likert scale (1,2,3,4,5).
2. In the dynamic analysis, a change equal to or higher than 0.33 points is considered as *relevant*. In this case, we chose a value representing 10% of our cutoff point from criterion 1 (3.33 points).

We are aware of the arbitrary choices; however, the chosen approach is simple and straight forward. Establishing a criterion is crucial to proceed with a clear interpretation of the data. The following table provides a summary of the answers on the research questions for each of the five firms. The figures in bold correspond to the most *relevant* values following the above-mentioned rubric. In the tables, *difference* stands for perceptions of differences between home country and host country along each psychic distance dimension, while *impact* refers to what extent managers perceive that each dimension affects their business with the host country.

Table 5 PD perceptions (pre- and post-entry static and dynamic analyses; variation between pre-entry and post-entry)

PD dimensions	Difference			Impact		
	Static analysis		Dynamic analysis	Static analysis		Dynamic analysis
	Pre-entry	Post-entry	Variation (%)	Pre-entry	Post-entry	Variation (%)
Geographical distance	**3.60**	**4.40**	**+0.80 (+22.2%)**	3	3.60	**+0.60 (+20%)**
Culture	**4**	**4.42**	**+0.42 (+10.50%)**	**3.83**	**3.80**	0.03 (+0.78%)
Language	**4.20**	**4.20**	0	**3.33**	**3.80**	**+0.47 (+14.11%)**
Level of education	2.80	2.80	0	2.50	2.24	−0.26 (−10.40%)
Level of technological development	3.20	3	−0.20 (−6.25%)	3.33	2.80	**−0.53** (−15.91%)
Level of economic development	3.40	2.60	**−0.80 (−23.52%)**	3.16	3	−0.16 (−5.06%)
Logistical infrastructure	2.60	3.20	**+0.6 (+23.07%)**	2.66	**3.60**	**+0.94** (+35.33%)
Political system	**4.20**	**4.60**	**+0.40 (+9.52%)**	**3.50**	**4.20**	**+0.70 (+20%)**
Legal system	**4.20**	**4.40**	+0.20 (+4.76%)	**3.66**	**4**	**+0.34 (+9.28%)**
Regulations	**4.60**	**4.60**	0	**3.83**	**4.20**	**+0.37 (+9.66%)**
Accepted business practices	**3.80**	**3.60**	−0.20 (−5.26%)	3	**3.60**	**+0.60 (+20%)**
Business ethics	**3.80**	**3.40**	**−0.40 (−10.52%)**	3	3.20	+0.20 (+6.66%)
Total average	**3.70**	**3.75**	**+0.5 (+13.51%)**	3.23	**3.50**	+0.27 (+8.35%)

Table 6 Most relevant PD dimensions in terms of perceived differences by Chinese managers between China and Germany and the perceived impact on the businesses (average values along 12 dimensions on the basis of the static analysis)

PD dimensions	Difference			Impact			Total
	Pre-entry	Post-entry	Average	Pre-entry	Post-entry	Average	Average (differences & impact)
Regulations	4.60	4.60	4.60	3.83	4.20	4	4.30
Legal system	4.20	4.40	4.30	3.66	4	3.83	4.06
Political system	4.20	4.60	4.40	3.50	4.20	3.85	4.12
Culture	4	4.20	4.10	3.83	3.80	3.81	3.95
Language	4	4.20	4.10	3.33	3.80	3.56	3.83
Geographical distance	3.60	4.40	4	3	3.60	3.30	3.65
Accepted business practices	3.80	3.60	3.70	3	3.60	3.30	3.50
Business ethics	3.80	3.40	3.60	3	3.20	3.10	3.35
Level of technological development	3.20	3	3.10	3.33	2.80	3.06	3.08
Level of economic development	3.40	2.60	3	3.16	3	3.08	3.04
Logistical infrastructure	2.60	3.20	2.90	2.66	3.60	3.13	3.01
Level of education	2.80	2.80	2.80	2.50	2.40	2.45	2.62
TOTAL AVERAGE	**3.68**	**3.75**	**3.71**	**3.23**	**3.51**	**3.37**	**3.54**

4.2 Cross-Case Analysis

The results of the static and the dynamic analyses of psychic distance perceptions are shown in Table 5 (differences between home country and host country and impact on the business in the host country along each dimension).

Table 7 Chinese managers' experiences (regulation-cluster dimensions: "regulations," "political system," "legal system")

Manager/company	Experience	PD perceptions of differences		Total of the average values	PD perceptions of impact		Total of the average values
		Pre-entry	Post-entry		Pre-entry	Post-entry	
SF Suntech Deutschland GmbH	- Yes (investments in countries other than Germany)	4	3.33	3.66	2.33	1.33	1.83
CEM Instruments (Germany) GmbH	- Yes (study abroad in a country other than Germany) - Yes (work and study in Germany)	4.66	5	4.83	4.66	4.66	4.66
TOTAL AVERAGE				4.24			3.24
Sunda renewable energy GmbH	No experience	4	5	4.50	5	5	5
Risen Energy GmbH		4	4.66	4.33	3	4.66	3.83
Sumec Europe GmbH		5	5	5	5	5	5
TOTAL AVERAGE				4.61			4.61

The data in Table 5 show that Chinese managers mostly perceive *differences* in regulation-cluster dimensions, i.e., "regulations" (4.60), "political system," and "legal system" (4.20 each) as well as "language" (4.20) *before* entering Germany, followed by the differences in "culture" (4.00), "accepted business practices," "business ethics," (both 3.80) and "geographical distance" (3.60). Unlike our research, Child et al. (2009) do not differentiate between pre- and post-entry perceptions. Our findings show that *after* the market entry, perceptions along the regulation-related psychic distance dimensions do not change significantly in comparison with the period *before* the market entry.

With respect to the *impact on the business* in Germany, "culture" and "regulations" (both 3.83), and "legal system" (3.66) are among the most significant psychic distance dimensions for our respondents *before* entering the market. Managers may become more aware of the actual importance for business of these dimensions in the post-market entry, *after* having their first experiences in the new environment. Publicly available information helps managers to assess the differences between countries on dimensions such as culture, language, legal and political systems without having concrete experiences (Child et al. 2009). But latest and most up-to-date information about business regulations and practices may be hard to gather before engaging with the host country. The results from the dynamic analysis (Table 5) show to which extent perceptions of the psychic distance dimensions change before and after entering the market. For instance, the perceived distance of "geographical distance" raises by 22.2% after the market entry, showing that managers realize the difference between China and Germany only after establishing a business in Germany.

Once in Germany, "culture" (+10.50%) and "political system" (+9.52%) are perceived as more relevant dimensions for doing businesses than previously expected. This means that some dimensions are overestimated in their impact on business before entering the market and some other dimensions are underestimated. However, psychic distance and its impact on business do not change over time along specific dimensions such as "level of education" and "regulations." Perceived difference in "business ethics" decreases after entering the German market (−10.52%). The perceived impact of "business ethics" on businesses does not change significantly after the market entry. Some other dimensions do not undergo any significant changes either and managers seem to be aware of their perceptions of impact toward certain dimensions such as "culture," "level of education," "level of economic development," and "business ethics" (Table 5).

According to these results, Chinese managers report higher psychic distance perceptions in terms of *differences* between China and Germany rather than perceptions of *impact* on their businesses. The analysis on the dynamics shows that, before entering the market, Chinese managers perceive larger differences along certain dimensions (e.g., *differences*: "accepted business practices," 3.80) and lower differences over others (e.g., *differences*: "political system" and "legal system," both 4.20). Only after entering the market, they realize that they may have overestimated or underestimated their psychic distance perceptions (e.g., *differences*: "logistical infrastructure" −23.07%; *impact*: "accepted business practices," +20%). They realize their relevance on their business only in the post-market entry and adjust their perceptions to the new foreign environment. As Table 6 shows, Chinese managers rated the differences of eight out of 12 dimensions as relevant (above the midpoint value 3.00). They further perceive that these dimensions have an impact on business (Table 6).

Qualitative data regarding the follow-up question on "regulations" confirm the high psychic distance perceptions along the regulation-cluster dimensions. In the current scenario, two main events are playing a determining role. As first, the financial crisis has resulted in a decrease in consumption incentives due to budget cuts. Second, antidumping policies imposed entry barriers to Chinese firms as a consequence of trade disputes between China and EU. According to our interviewees: *"Germany is also an important market of solar panels. In order to guarantee a competitive market, the EU imposed antidumping measures on imports from China.* There is a minimum import price agreement which was supposed to expire on December 2015. Then the EU has extended this deadline for one year". As far as the regulation-cluster dimension is concerned, *"antidumping is not only an economic issue but also a policy issue to keep the balance between China and Europe relationships"*. Table 7 shows that three out of five Chinese managers neither had previous work and study experiences in Germany nor had experiences with FDI before their investment in Germany.

4.3 Propositions

Referring to the main findings of this chapter, we drew up the following propositions:

Proposition 1

a) *Chinese managers perceive (and are aware of) differences between China and Germany on the regulation-related cluster dimensions, i.e. "regulations", "legal system", and "political system". They are aware of their impact on business within the host country. "Culture", "language", "geographical distance" and "accepted business practices" are perceived by Chinese managers as less significant.*
b) *Managers' PD perceptions of differences between the "political systems" of the home and the host country is higher after the market-entry in comparison to the pre-market perceptions. Perceptions increase over time. Managers' perceptions of the impact of differences between the political systems on the actual business is increasing significantly from pre- to post-market entry. Hence, managers change their mind about the differences of the political systems and they think that this has a relevant impact on the business.*
c) *Managers' PD perceptions of differences between the "legal systems" of home and host country is higher in the post-market period than in the pre-market entry. However, perceptions of impact of these differences between the legal systems on the businesses does not change significantly over time.*
d) *Managers perceive high differences between "regulations" of the home and the host country. Perceptions of impact of regulations on businesses are slightly lower. In both cases—differences and impact—there are no changes over time from before entering the market in comparison to the period after the market entry in terms of differences while there is a slight variation over time in terms of impact of regulations on the business.*

Proposition 2

a) *The changes in Chinese managers' PD perceptions between China and Germany from pre- to post-market entry are moderated by work, study and investment experiences in the host country or abroad.*

b) *Along the regulation-related cluster dimensions—"regulations", "political system", and "legal system"—Chinese managers with no international experiences perceive high impact and differences, while Chinese managers with experiences perceive impact and differences as relatively low.*

5 Discussion

Chinese managers are expected to perceive psychic distance between China and Germany, since the two countries do objectively differ along the 12 analyzed psychic distance dimensions. Building on Child et al. (2002, 2009) specific items/dimensions of distance, we analyzed their relevance in the context of Chinese OFDI to Germany in the RE sector. Furthermore, following up Vaccarini et al.'s (2015) findings, we consider that perceptions of psychic distance might change between the pre-market entry and post-market entry. We conducted a "static" analysis and "dynamics" analysis of psychic distance dimensions, referring to two particular points of time, i.e., pre-entry and post-entry. We found that the regulation-cluster dimensions, and "culture," "language," "geographical distance," and "accepted business practices" are perceived as significantly distant by Chinese managers.

Child et al.'s (2002) study on the internationalization of Hong Kong firms indicated that "culture" was the most relevant element in creating distance and most important in impacting business. In Child et al.'s subsequent study (2009), the most important dimensions behind cultural dimension were "level of economic development," "level of education," and "level of technological development." Our study only partially confirms Child et al.'s (2002) observations. "Culture" is among the most relevant dimensions in our analysis, but followed by "language," geographical distance," and "accepted business practices." Next to "culture," we identified six dimensions as the most relevant ones in Child et al.'s (2009) PD-item list. Chinese managers perceive that the main gaps between China and Germany are related to the differences in regulations, political systems, legal systems, culture, language, geographical distance, and business practices. They also perceive that these dimensions affect their operational activities and their businesses with Germany.

Our results further show that some psychic distance dimensions that were scored quite high by Chinese managers in relation to perceived differences between Germany and China were not perceived to have a correspondent high impact on their businesses (Table 6). This is consistent with Child et al.'s (2009) study. For example, according to their findings, psychic distance perceptions of "culture" did not correspond to the perceived impact that culture has on the business. Table 6 shows the importance of psychic distance in terms of perceived differences between China and Germany (3.71) rather than psychic distance perceived impact on the business with Germany (3.37). The relevance of the psychic distance dimensions proposed by Child et al. (2009) is confirmed for the average values related to the perceptions of differences since they overcome our pre-defined threshold of 3.33 points (on the five-point Likert scale). The proposed operationalization of psychic distance can be considered a valuable framework to conduct analyses in IB regarding psychic distance, both in terms of perceived differences between home country and host country and perceived impact on the business with the host country. The overall results confirm proposition 1 regarding the relevance of psychic distance.

In Child et al.'s (2009) study, conducted on British companies exporting to Brazil, it is argued that information about regulations and business practices may not be obtained in advance, before gathering experiences in the host country. Our findings show the peculiar case of a "regulation-cluster dimension": Chinese managers in the RE sector perceive high differences in regulation-related dimensions between China and Germany. They seem to have higher concerns about regulations after gaining knowledge in the market and also after they gather actual experience in the post-market entry phase. In this case, experience seems to play an important role in moderating the perceived impact that regulations have on businesses. Managers seem to realize their increased perceptions along "political system" after entering the market (+20%).

Before entering the market, psychic distance perceptions of "geographical distance," "culture," "logistical Infrastructure," "political system," and "legal system" were underestimated if comparing them with the perceptions after entering the market. For instance, "geographical" distance and "logistical infrastructure" increase by 22.2% and 23.07%, respectively. On the contrary, "level of economic development" and "business ethics" decrease by 23.07% and 10.52% from the pre-entry to the post-entry, respectively. "Accepted business practices" was perceived to affect the business in the host country only after managers made their experiences in the market (increasing variation, 20%). Child et al. (2002) argue that previous experience in a given international location is a strategic bridging factor. Conversely, Williams and Grégoire (2015) focus on the pre-entry market information in terms of "prior knowledge" and its moderating role regarding perceptions and considerations of differences.

In our chapter, we follow Child et al.'s (2002) considerations regarding managers' previous experience and its moderating role on psychic distance perceptions. According to our findings (Table 7), managers who neither have previous work and study experience nor dealt with prior investments abroad have higher perceptions of differences (4.61) than the experienced ones (4.24) along the regulation-cluster. With respect to this, our results are consistent with proposition n. 2a and 2b. Accordingly, the less these experiences, the higher the perceptions of differences and the higher the perceived impact on business in general. The generalization out of our multiple case study is limited to the RE industry and to the context of Chinese OFDI to Germany. Given that the analyses conducted in this multiple case study are industry specific, the "regulatory" dimensions might be RE-specific. Further research should conduct analyses with a broader population of firms and countries.

6 Conclusion and Policy Implications

There is no question that China and Germany are different in many aspects, such as culture, language, business ethics, policy-making, and regulations. It is a logical consequence that these differences are supposed to be reflected by managers who do business with these two countries. These differences affect foreign direct investment (FDI) decisions by managers, in particular in the renewable energy sector, which has country-specific regulations and which is highly affected by constantly changing policies. The purpose of our chapter was to examine Chinese managers' perceptions of psychic distance (PD) between their home country and Germany and the impact of psychic distance perceptions on conduction business in the renewable energy (RE) sector. Because the RE sector is highly influenced by changing regulations, we particularly focused on regulation-related psychic distance dimensions, i.e., "regulations," "political system," and "legal system." Further, we surveyed the changes of Chinese managers' psychic distance perceptions before entering the German market for the first time by the means of FDI and after entering the market. This enabled us to identify ex ante misperceptions by Chinese managers and their possible corrections of these misperceptions over time. Our research results are highly relevant for practitioners, policy makers, and scholars:

We identified that Chinese managers misperceive the relevance and the impact of differences between various psychic distance dimensions (such as culture, policy-making, and regulation). Further studies show that this applies also to European executives doing business in China (Lv and Spigarelli 2015). We further found that managers, who are internationally inexperienced, misperceive differences among their home country and the host country and their impact on business to a higher degree than experienced managers. Hence, manager's perceptions are getting more accurate over time and experiences, and learning curves can be observed. This is not surprising. However, as we found in our analysis that misperceptions can be identified not only for inexperienced managers but also for experienced managers, extensive executive training to inform managers about differences between countries and their impact on businesses in the host country seem to be necessary to avoid failures in FDI. Probably this finding is also not surprising. Nevertheless, our data show that managers are not well (enough) prepared for their duties in the foreign country. This seems to be especially true for FDI in the RE sector, because of constantly changing rules and regulations in this relatively young sector. Further research should show if this is particularly an issue of FDI from emerging markets to developed countries, or if the described effects are country or industry specific.

Our findings are also highly relevant for policy makers, in particular in the RE sector. As rules and regulations in the relatively new RE sector constantly change, differences in policy-making, legal systems, regulations between the countries are the result. To a certain degree, managers seem not to be aware of this fact and on the subsequent consequences on their business. Industry-related host country institutions may consider to take more explicit actions to explain foreign investors their industry-specific policies and regulations and to their impact on business success.

Our findings build on Child et al.'s (2009) studies on psychic distance and affirm the relevance of 12 psychic distance dimensions. Eight of these dimensions are (most) significant and among them are the regulation-related dimensions. Manager's perceptions of impact along the "political system" increase significantly after the market entry. This means that managers underestimated its relevance in the pre-market entry period. They seem to realize after the market entry that the regulation-related dimensions have higher impact on their businesses than previously estimated, before entering the market. Thus, next to the operationalization strategies that have been applied by IB scholars so far, future studies should look at the dynamics of psychic distance perceptions over time and differentiate between pre-market entry phase and post-market entry phase.

Notes

1. This research is part of the EU-funded project is POREEN—*Partnering Opportunities between Europe and China in the Renewable Energies and Environmental iNdustries*. With its multi-disciplinary approach, it gathers legal experts, engineers, and economist. The aim is to investigate a number of aspects of Chinese and Europe integration in the environmental and green tech sectors. 1) "This project is funded by the European Union under the Marie Curie Action's IRSES". 2) "This

publication does not necessarily reflect the opinion of the EU" [When relevant]. The research leading to these results has received funding from the People Programme (Marie Curie Actions) of the European Union's Seventh Framework Programme FP7/2007-2013/under REA grant agreement n° 318908.

2. The company covers the following areas: Germany, mainland China, Hong Kong, and Singapore (http://www.melchersraffel.com/de/).
3. Intersolar Europe international fair, Munich, June 2015.
4. Questionnaire available here:https://docs.google.com/forms/d/1LCXei5edMbskRrlylFslGyi7M9PrGPnfHptlVgUkdZg/viewform?c=0&w=1.

References

Ahonen, P., Tienari, J., & Vaara, E. (2011). There is no alternative"—or is there? A critical case study approach for international business research. In R. Piekkari & C. Welch (Eds.), *Rethinking the case study in international business research* (pp. 85–106). Cheltenham: Edward Elgar.

Beckerman, W. (1956). Distance and the pattern of intra-European trade. *The Review of Economics and Statistics, 38*(31), 31–40.

Brewer, M. B. (2003). *Intergroup relations*. Berkshire: Free University Press.

Brewer, P. (2007). Psychic distance and Australian export market selection. *Australian Journal of Management, 32*(1), 73–94.

Brouthers, K. D. (2002). Institutional, cultural and transaction cost influences on entry mode choice and performance. *Journal of International Business Studies, 33*(2), 203–221.

Buckley, P. J., Clegg, L. J., Cross, A. R., Liu, X., Voss, H., & Zheng, P. (2007). The determinants of Chinese outward foreign direct investment. *Journal of International Business Studies, 38*(4), 499–518.

Campbell, J. T., Eden, L., & Miller, S. R. (2012). Multinationals and corporate social responsibility in host countries: Does distance matter? *Journal of International Business Studies, 43*(1), 84–106.

Caprar, D. V., Devinney, T. M., Kirkman, B. L., & Caligiuri, P. (2015). Conceptualizing and measuring culture in international business and management: From challenges to potential solutions. *Journal of International Business Studies, 46*(9), 1011–1027.

Cheng, L. K., & Ma, Z. (2008). China's outward foreign direct investment. In *China's Growing Role in World Trade*. Chicago: University of Chicago Press.

http://www.isid.ac.in/~psu/seminar/12_12_2008_Paper.doc. Accessed Apr 2017.
Cheung, Y. W., & Qian, X. (2009). Empirics of China's outward direct investment. *Pacific Economic Review, 14*(3), 312–341.
Child, J., Ng, S. H., & Wong, C. (2002). Psychic distance and internationalization: Evidence from Hong Kong Firms. *International Studies of Management & Organization, 32,* 36–56.
Child, J., Rodrigues, S. B., & Frynas, J. G. (2009). Psychic distance, its impact and coping modes: Interpretations of SMEs decision-makers. *Management International Review, 49*(2), 199–224.
Curran, L. (2015). The impact of trade policy on global production networks: The solar panel case. *Review of International Political Economy, 22*(5), 1025–1054. http://dx.doi.org/10.1080/09692290.2015.1014927. Accessed Apr 2017.
Curran, L., Lv, P., & Spigarelli, F. (2016). Chinese investment in the EU renewable energy sector: Motives, impediments and policy implications. *Energy Policy*, forthcoming.
Dow, D. (2000). A note on psychological distance and export market selection. *Journal of International Marketing, 8*(1), 51–64.
Eisenhardt, K. M. (1989). Building theories from case study research. *Academy of Management Review, 14,* 532–550.
Eisenhardt, K. M. (2009). Origin of alliance portfolios: Entrepreneurs, network strategies, and firm performance. *Academy of Management Journal, 52*(2), 246–279.
Evans, J., Treadgold, A., & Mavondo, F. T. (2000). Explaining export development through psychic distance. *International Marketing Review, 17*(2), 164–168.
Fairclough, N. (1993). Critical discourse analysis and the marketization of public discourse: The universities. *Discourse and Society, 4*(2), 133–168.
German Federal Foreign Office. (2015). *China.* http://www.auswaertiges-amt.de/sid_4DB22E9755703CC3A81EF09DB47D67C6/EN/Aussenpolitik/Laender/Laenderinfos/01-Nodes/China_node.html#doc474918bodyText4. Accessed Apr 2017.
Gruber, W. H., & Vernon, R. (1970). The technology factor in a world trade matrix. In R. Vernon (Ed.), *The Technology Factor in International Trade* (pp. 233–272). New York: National Bureau of Economic Research.
Harzing, A. W. (2003). The role of culture in entry-mode studies: From neglect to myopia? In J. L. C. Cheng & M. A. Hitt (Eds.), *Managing*

multinationals in a knowledge economy: Economics culture. Advances in International Management, Vol. 15 (pp. 75–127). Bingley: Emerald Group.

Hashim, F. (2012). Outward internationalization and FDI: Motives for Malaysian MNEs moving into China. *Review of Business & Finance Studies, 3*(2), 89–102.

Hertenstein, P., Sutherland, D., & Anderson, J. (2015). Internationalization within networks: Exploring the relationship between inward and outward FDI in China's auto components industry. *Asia Pacific Journal of Management, 34*(1), 69–96.

Johanson, J., & Vahlne, E. (1977). The internationalization process of the firm: A model of knowledge development and increasing foreign market commitments. *Journal of International Business Studies, 8*(1), 23–32.

Johanson, J., & Wiedersheim-Paul, F. (1975). The internationalization of the firm: Four swedish case studies. *The Journal of Management Studies, 12*(3), 305–323.

Kogut, B., & Singh, H. (1988). The effect of national culture on the choice of entry mode. *Journal of International Business Studies, 19*(3), 411–432.

Kolstad, I., & Wiig, A. (2012). What determines Chinese outward FDI? *Journal of World Business, 47*(1), 26–34.

Lau, H. F. (2003). Industry evolution and internationalization processes of firms from a newly industrialized economy. *Journal of Business Research, 56*(10), 847–852.

Lecraw, D. (1977). Direct investment by firms from less developed countries. *Oxford Economic Papers, 29*(3), 442–457.

Leamer, E. E. (1974). The commodity composition of international trade in manufactures: An empirical analysis. *Oxford Economic Papers, 26*(3), 350–374.

Linnemann, H. (1966). *An econometric study of international trade flows*. Amsterdam: North-Holland Publishing Company.

Luo, Y., & Tung, R. L. (2007). International expansion of emerging market enterprises: A springboard perspective. *Journal of International Business Studies, 38*(4), 481–498.

Luo, Y., & Wang, S. L. (2012). Foreign direct investment strategies by developing country multinationals: A diagnostic model for home country effects. *Global Strategy Journal, 2*(3), 244–261.

Lv, P., & Spigarelli, F. (2015). The integration of Chinese and European renewable energy markets: The role of Chinese foreign direct investments. *Energy Policy, 81*, 14–26.

Lv, P., & Spigarelli, F. (2016). The determinants of location choice: Chinese foreign direct investments in the European renewable energy sector. *International Journal of Emerging Markets*, Vol. 4 (forthcoming).

Magnusson, P., & Boyle, B. (2005). Psychic distance: A review of empirical research from 1988 to 2004. *Academy of International Business Annual Meeting*, Quebec. https://aib.msu.edu/events/2005/aib_2005_proceedings.pdf. Accessed Apr 2017.

Nordström, K. A., & Vahlne, J. E. (1994). *Is the globe shrinking? Psychic distance and the establishment of swedish sales subsidiaries during the last 100 years, international trade: Regional and global issues* (pp. 41–56). New York: St. Martin's Press.

Peng, M. W., Wang, D. Y. L., & Jiang, Y. (2008). An institution-based view of international business strategy: A focus on emerging economies. *Journal of International Business Studies, 39*(5), 920–936.

Powell, M., & Ansic, D. (1997). Gender differences in risk behavior in financial decision-making: An experimental analysis. *Journal of Economic Psychology, 18*(6), 605–628.

Puri, M., Tavoletti, E., & Cerruti C. (2015). Business model innovation in emerging economies: Leveraging institutional voids. In: La Rovere, O., de Jesus M. (Eds.), Entrepreneurship in BRICS: Policy and Research to Support Entrepreneurs (pp. 143–162), Dordrecht: Springer; Boston: Kluwer Academic Publishers.

Puthussery, P. N., Child, J., & Rodrigues, S. B. (2014). Psychic distance, its business impact and modes of coping: A study of British and Indian partner SMEs. *Management International Review, 54,* 1–29.

Rugman, A. M., & Chang, H. O. (2008). The international competitiveness of Asian firms. *Journal of Strategy and Management, 1*(1), 57–71.

Salomon, R., & Wu, Z. (2012). Institutional distance and local isomorphism strategy. *Journal of International Business Studies, 43*(4), 343–367.

Shenkar, O. (2001). Cultural distance revisited: Towards a more rigorous conceptualization and measurement of cultural differences. *Journal of International Business Studies, 32*(3), 519–535.

Shenkar, O. (2012). Cultural distance revisited. *Journal of International Business Studies, 43*(1), 1–11.

Simon, H. A. (1979). Rational decision making in business organizations. *American Economic Review, 69*(4), 493–513.

Sousa, C. M., & Bradley, F. (2006). Cultural distance and psychic distance: Two peas in a pod? *Journal of International Marketing, 14*(1), 49–70.

Stoian, C. (2013). Extending Dunning's investment development path: The role of home country institutional determinants in explaining outward foreign direct investment. *International Business Review, 22*(3), 615–637.

Stottinger, B., & Schlegelmilch, B. B. (1998). Explaining export development through psychic distance: Enlightening or elusive? *International Marketing Review, 15*(5), 357–372.

Stöttinger, B., & Schlegelmilch, B. B. (2000). Psychic distance: A concept past its due date? *International Marketing Review, 17*(2), 169–173.

Tajfel, H., & Wilkes, A. L. (1963). Classification and quantitative judgment. *British Journal of Psychology, 54,* 101–114.

Tajfel, H., & Turner, J. C. (1979). An integrative theory of intergroup conflict. In W. G. Austin & S. Worchel (Eds.), *The social psychology of intergroup relations* (pp. 33–47). Monterey, CA: Brooks/Cole.

Turner, J. C. (1975). Social comparison and social identity: Some prospects for intergroup behaviour. *European Journal of Social Psychology, 5,* 5–34.

Vaccarini, K., Spigarelli, F., & Tavoletti, E. (2015). European green tech FDI in China: The role of culture, c.MET Working Papers 1507, c.MET-05—Centro Interuniversitario di Economia Applicata alle Politiche per L'industria, lo Sviluppo locale e l'Internazionalizzazione. https://socionet.ru/publication.xml?h=repec:cme:wpaper:1507&l=en. Accessed Apr 2017.

Van Dijk, T. A. (2000). *Ideology and discourse a multidisciplinary introduction.* Barcelona: Pompeu Fabra University.

Wei, W. X., & Alon, I. (2010). Chinese outward direct investment: A study on macroeconomic determinants. *International Journal of Business and Emerging Markets, 2*(4), 352–369.

Wells, L. (1983). *Third world multinationals: The role of foreign direct investment from developing countries.* Cambridge: MIT Press.

Wilder, D. A. (1978). Perceiving persons as a group: Effects on attribution of causality and beliefs. *Social Psychology, 41*(1), 13–23.

Williams, D. W., & Grégoire, D. A. (2015). Seeking commonalities or avoiding differences? Re-conceptualizing distance and its effects on internationalization decisions. *Journal of International Business Studies, 46*(3), 253–284.

Xu, D., & Shenkar, O. (2002). Institutional distance and the multinational enterprise. *Academy of Management Review, 27*(4), 608–618.

Yin, R. K. (2003). *Case study research: Design and methods* (3rd ed.). Thousand Oaks, CA: Sage.

Zaheer, S., Schomaker, M. S., & Nachum, L. (2012). Distance without direction: Restoring credibility to a much-loved construct. *Journal of International Business Studies, 43,* 18–27.

Zhou, M. (2006). The Chinese Diaspora and international migration. In Y. Bian, C. Kwok-Bun, & C. Tak-Sing (Eds.), *Social transformations in Chinese societies*. Leiden, Netherlands: Brill Academic Publishers.

6
Summary Conclusions

Abstract This book aimed to analyze the concept of psychic distance in international ventures. The construct was explored in its definition and operationalized in the context of Sino-European FDI. More specifically, the analysis was conducted on an industry level with a focus on the green tech sector.

Keywords PD · Psychic distance · International ventures · Definition Operationalization · Sino-European FDI · Industry level · Green tech sector

The multi-dimensional psychic distance construct elaborated by international business scholars (Child et al. 2009) enabled to explore its single components and how managers perceive them. "Culture" was one of the most relevant dimensions according to data.

As for its conceptualization, Child et al.'s (2009: 201) definition of psychic distance was adopted in this book. Psychic distance is defined as "the distance that is *perceived* to exist between characteristics of a firm's home country and a foreign country with which that firm is, or is contemplating, doing business or investing." Next to the conceptualization,

K. Vaccarini et al., *Cultural Distance in International Ventures*,
DOI 10.1007/978-3-319-62193-7_6

the same authors' (Child et al. 2009) operationalization of the concept was also adopted and applied in the context of Sino–European foreign direct investments in the green tech industry. Accordingly, psychic distance is composed of 12 dimensions, which stem from recent specific-theoretical frameworks and empirical works carried out in the international business literature. In particular, the "GLOBE" framework (Ghemawat 2001) for measuring "distances" between countries and Child et al.'s (2002, 2009) studies constitute the cornerstones of how psychic distance was conceptualized, operationalized, and applied in this book. Not only perceptions of *differences* along each of the 12 dimensions were detected but also the *impact* perceived by managers on each dimension on the business with the host country.

Next to international business, social psychological theoretical foundations were explored and adopted in this book. This interdisciplinary approach enabled to interpret the phenomena under examination (perceptions of psychic distance and culture) from different perspectives. Integrating different discipline areas provides a more comprehensive overview on the object of the study. Not only combination of disciplines but also their complementarity plays a crucial role in terms of synergy. This book draws upon social psychology literature and explores managers' perceptions of psychic distance and culture. Studies on perceptions conducted by international business scholars (e.g., Stöttinger and Schlegelmilch 1998) are based on the principles of cognition. Social psychologists show that individuals tend to prefer familiar situations rather than unfamiliar ones (e.g., Powell and Ansic 1997), thus, this book tried to incorporate the literature on distance and perceptions by adopting an interdisciplinary approach and relying on international business and social psychology (Sumner 1906; Turner 1975; Brewer 2003).

We investigate of non-economic factors determining FDI location decisions by adopting an interdisciplinary perspective of analysis. This work goes beyond country and firm level analyses; it focuses on the individual level and on the "psychic" side of the concept. Prior studies seemed to have lacked of considering the individual and cognitive part of the construct (e.g., Hofstede 1980; Dow 2000; Dow and Karunaratna 2006). This study encouraged to use a more qualitative approach to capture the various facets of psychic distance with its 12 dimensions.

The context of Sino-European FDI is the business setting of each chapter composing this book and it contributes to have in-depth insights into a single sector, the green tech industry. The need for scholars to conduct industry level analyses is widely recognized in international business literature (e.g., Lv and Spigarelli 2016). In recent years, the combination of the increasing environmental awareness in China and the economic recession in Europe has created a climate, which has registered an increase of FDI flows between China and Europe (and vice versa) in the green tech industry (Lv and Spigarelli 2016). China has been devoting increasing attention to environmental issues and pollution reduction thanks to the "green policy" embedded in the recent Five-Year Plans (Langer and Watson 2004; Aiwa and Yang 2010; Huang and Chen 2015).

The four chapters of this book aimed at in-depth exploring the psychic distance concept by detecting the perceived *differences* between home and host country along its dimensions as well as the perceived *impact* that these dimensions have on the business with the host country. In short, after the introductory part, Chap. 2 provides an overview on the debate of psychic distance and its role as a non-economic determinant for FDI location decisions. Among the psychic distance dimensions, culture was considered one of the most relevant. It was further investigated in the form of conceptual study (Chap. 3) and multiple-case study (Chap. 4). Next to this, a differentiation in perceptions between two phases of the internationalization process emerged: pre—and post-market entry (Chap. 5). Psychic distance perceptions of managers change overtime from before the market entry to the period after that. This chapter illustrates the extent to which perceptions vary overtime in relation to each dimension, both in terms of *differences* between home and host country and in terms of *impact* on the businesses with the host country. Perceptions and understandings of managers represent the core of the construct since their perceptions and skills in overcoming psychic distance are consequential for the firms' internationalization (e.g., Evans et al. 2000).

The contributions of this book can be summarized as follows. This work confirms the relevance of psychic distance in international business settings and the relevance of the tools used to detect it. 6 out of 12 psychic distance dimensions are important for managers, especially culture, political system, legal system, and regulations. Differentiating between pre—and the post-market entry perceptions by conducting *static* and *dynamic* analyses may add value to the operationalization of psychic distance, enriching the already available model in the international business literature. Firstly, the static and dynamic analyses conducted in Chap. 5 provided an in-depth insight on the (mis)match between managers' perceptions of psychic distance in two points in time, the pre- and the post-market entry. Secondly, these analyses enable to detect on which dimensions managers engaging in international business activities should focus and work on before entering the foreign market.

This research confirmed the relevance of culture in international business contexts as well as political system, legal system, and regulations. As about the role of cultural perceptions of European managers toward China, main findings show that they seem not to take into account intra-China regional differences before entering the market as far as cultural aspects is concerned. Thus, the need for regional tailored studies is confirmed, according to recent trends in literature. Main findings show the relevance for differentiating the internationalization phases in "pre-" and "post-market entry" when analyzing individual perceptions of psychic distance and culture. They also show the moderating role of managers' "prior experiences" affecting the variation of perceptions (*differences* and *impact*).

These results have several implications. At policy level, for the EU, findings show the factors creating obstacles and "distance" between Europe and China as well as between China and its host European countries (the case of Germany was investigated). Managers' perceptions of their host countries should be considered not only at industry and policy level so that they can be aligned with FDI attraction policies but also at regional level (intra-China). At policy level, for China and EU, results show how relevant is to invest in decreasing cultural barriers and on other crucial factors and dimensions which hinder the practical business operation activities (political system, legal system, and regulations) not only after but also before the market entry.

As last point of this final remark, it is necessary to merge the insights acquired from both discipline areas which were explored in this book: international business and—though more marginally—social psychology. The relevance of the psychic distance construct can be confirmed thanks to the relevance of 6 out of 12 dimensions. As far as its operationalization is concerned, this book contributed in adding two specific types of analyses by differentiating a pre- and post-market entry phase. These analyses can be conducted when exploring the concept in international business settings: the static and the dynamic analyses. Specifically, by investigating the dynamics of perceptions in-depth insights on how the psychic distance dimensions are perceived by managers emerge not only after but also before the market entry. For example, preventive actions on "regulations" can be adopted in order to better prepare managers in facing "regulations"—related issues.

According to data, perceptions of differences and impact do not report the same values. A social psychological perspective of analysis may help to work on differences in terms of how to approach them and how to generate value out of them. Managers can work on differences by taking part in intercultural trainings so that they can be prepared on how to cope with them. This work can be done at cognitive level, by raising managers' awareness on the potential embedded in those differences. The intercultural laboratory illustrated in Chap. 3 served this purpose. It enables to work at cognitive level, by going beyond perceptions and understanding the sociocognitive dynamics behind them. A social psychological perspective would help in using a certain terminology to foster positivity and synergies when home and host countries are involved. For example, scholars in this area focus on "cultural differences" when speaking about home and host country diversities. Capitalizing on these differences is possible, depending on how to approach them. International business scholars rather refer to the concept of "psychic distance," which contains a certain idea of "distance" per se. A negative meaning is embedded when using this terminology and may lead to emphasize diversities.

Data show that prior managers' experience has a moderating role on how managers perceive the psychic distance dimensions. Inexperienced managers report higher perceptions of impact than the experienced ones. Integrating both "prior experiences" and intercultural training would be optimal for preparing managers in dealing with psychic distance. This would help to prevent negative perceptions of differences between home and host country and negative perceptions of impact on the businesses. Preventive actions on the dimensions reporting higher or lower values of perceptions can be taken at policy level.

References

Aiwa, M., & Yang, C. (2010). Green credit, green stimulus, green revolution? China's mobilization of banks for environmental cleanup. *The Journal of Environment and Development, 19*(2), 119–144.

Brewer, M. B. (2003). *Intergroup relations.* Berkshire: Free University Press.

Child, J., Ng, S. H., & Wong, C. (2002). Psychic distance and internationalization: Evidence from Hong Kong firms. *International Studies of Management and Organization, 32*(1), 36–56.

Child, J., Rodrigues, S. B., & Frynas, J. G. (2009). Psychic distance, its impact and coping modes: Interpretations of SMEs decision-makers. *Management International Review, 49*(2), 199–224.

Dow, D. (2000). A note on psychological distance and export market selection. *Journal of International Marketing, 8*(1), 51–64.

Dow, D., & Karunaratna, A. (2006). Developing a multidimensional instrument to measure psychic distance stimuli. *Journal of International Business Studies, 37*(5), 578–602.

Evans, J., Treadgold, A., & Mavondo, F. T. (2000). Psychic distance and the performance of international retailers–a suggested theoretical framework. *International Marketing Review, 17*(4/5), 373–391.

Ghemawat, P. (2001). Distance still matters. *Harvard Business Review, 79*(8), 137–147.

Hofstede, G. (1980). *Culture's consequences: International differences in work-related values.* Beverly Hills, CA: Sage.

Huang, R., & Chen, D. (2015). Does environmental information disclosure benefit waste discharge reduction? Evidence from China. *Journal of Business Ethics, 129*(3), 535–552.

Langer, K., & Watson, R. (2004). The greening of China's building industry. *China Business Review, 31*(6), 56–63.

Lv, P., & Spigarelli, F. (2016). The determinants of location choice: Chinese foreign direct investments in the European renewable energy sector. *International Journal of Emerging Markets*, forthcoming, 333–356.

Powell, M., & Ansic, D. (1997). Gender differences in risk behavior in financial decision-making: An experimental analysis. *Journal of Economic Psychology, 18*(6), 605–628.

Stöttinger, B., & Schlegelmilch, B. B. (1998). Explaining export development through psychic distance: enlightening or elusive?. *International Marketing Review, 15*(5), 357–372.

Sumner, W. G. (1906). *Folksways*. New York: Ginn.

Turner, J. C. (1975). Social comparison and social identity: Some prospects for intergroup behaviour. *European Journal of Social Psychology, 5*, 5–34.

7
Appendix

Abstract For the purpose of this book, two questionnaires were submitted to our managers. The first one was addressed to the European managers representing their companies investing in China. The second one was addressed to Chinese managers investing in Europe.

Keywords Questionnaire · Interview · Psychic distance model

For the purpose of this book, two questionnaires were submitted to our managers. The first one was addressed to the European managers representing their companies investing in China. The second one was addressed to Chinese managers investing in Europe, more specifically, in Germany.

We focused our interviews on the psychic distance model (Child et al. 2009) (Table 1) included in both questionnaires. Nevertheless, the presence of all the other questions enabled us to have a more comprehensive overview of the contexts under examination. Child et al.'s (2009) model provided in-depth insights into the topics of psychic distance and culture, which resulted to be the most relevant dimension according to our respondents.

K. Vaccarini et al., *Cultural Distance in International Ventures*,
DOI 10.1007/978-3-319-62193-7_7

Table 1 Psychic distance model (Adapted from Child et al. 2009)

PD dimensions	Degree of *difference* between home country and host country	Extent to which it *impacts* on my business with the host country
Geographical distance		
Culture		
Language		
Level of education		
Level of technological development		
Level of economic development		
Logistic infrastructure		
Political system		
Legal system		
Regulations		
Accepted business practices		
Business ethics		

1 = "no real difference"/" does not impact on my business at all"
5 = "very great difference"/" impacts on my business very much"

In order to detect perceptions of psychic distance, managers were introduced to above table (Table 1), which lists 12 kinds of "distances." They were asked how much *difference* they perceived along each dimension between their home and host country and to what extent these dimensions *impact* on their business with the host country. The grading was based on a 5-point Likert scale.

The focus on perceptions in this book fills the void of previous studies on psychic distance, which have focused on differences between countries and failed to examine the cognition of decision-makers in any depth (Stöttinger and Schlegelmilch 2000). Previous studies relied on questionnaire survey data (e.g., Klein and Roth 1990), experts (e.g., Dow 2000), or national indicators (e.g., Dow and Karunaratna 2006) limiting their attention to the "psychic" side of the concept (Child et al. 2009). Perceptions and understandings of decision-makers represent the core of psychic distance (Evans et al. 2000) since their perceptions and skills in overcoming psychic distance are crucial in the firms' internationalization process.

Child et al.'s (2009) psychic distance model adopted in this research is derived from prior empirical and theoretical studies conducted by the same authors and by other international business scholars. First, it was applied in a study aimed at re-examining the concept of psychic distance in the internationalization process of the firms (Child et al. 2002). In this work, the authors examined the possible mix of factors and attributes linked to the psychic distance dimensions and construct. Secondly, it was applied in a later study regarding managers in British companies with a business interest in Brazil (Child et al. 2009). This is the work applied to our Sino-European context and explained throughout this book. Both studies relied on a multiple-case study design.

The empirical origin of the 12 dimensions can be found in the international business literature, especially the Nordic studies (Johanson and Vahlne 1977), and in the main findings of Child et al.'s (2009) research conducted in 2002. As about the theoretical origin, Ghemawat's (2001) "CAGE" classification of distance constitutes the overall framework of the 12 dimensions. This is quite a comprehensive classification of distance between two countries along cultural, administrative, geographic, and economic factors. Accordingly, "cultural distance includes differences in language and social norms, administrative distance included differences in political system, government policies and institutions, and economic distance includes differences in income levels, infrastructure, human and other resources" (Child et al. 2009: 204–205).

References

Child, J., Ng, S. H., & Wong, C. (2002). Psychic distance and internationalization: Evidence from Hong Kong firms. *International Studies of Management and Organization, 32*(1), 36–56.

Child, J., Rodrigues, S. B., & Frynas, J. G. (2009). Psychic distance, its impact and coping modes: Interpretations of SMEs decision-makers. *Management International Review, 49*(2), 199–224.

Dow, D. (2000). A note on psychological distance and export market selection. *Journal of International Marketing, 8*(1), 51–64.

Dow, D., & Karunaratna, A. (2006). Developing a multidimensional instrument to measure psychic distance stimuli. *Journal of International Business Studies, 37*(5), 578–602.

Evans, Treadgold, & Mavondo, F. T. (2000). Psychic distance and the performance of international retailers. A suggested theoretical framework. *International Marketing Review, 17*(4/5), 373–391.

Ghemawat, P. (2001). Distance still matters. *Harvard Business Review, 79*(8), 137–147.

Johanson, J., & Vahlne, E. (1977). The internationalization process of the firm: A model of knowledge development and increasing foreign market commitments. *Journal of International Business Studies, 8,* 23–32.

Klein, S., & Roth, V. J. (1990). Determinants of export channel structure: The effects of experience and psychic distance reconsidered. *International Marketing Review, 7*(5), 27–38.

Stöttinger, B., & Schlegelmilch, B. B. (2000). Psychic distance: A concept past its due date? *International Marketing Review, 17*(2), 169–173.

Index

K. Vaccarini et al., *Cultural Distance in International Ventures*,
DOI 10.1007/978-3-319-62193-7

The manufacturer's authorised representative in the EU is Springer Nature Customer Service Centre GmbH, Europaplatz 3, 69115 Heidelberg, Germany. If you have any concerns regarding our products, please contact ProductSafety@springernature.com

Printed and bound by CPI Group (UK) Ltd, Croydon, CR0 4YY
25/09/2026
02222890-0018